H.F. Mytton,   Borderer

Hunting and Sporting Notes in the West Midlands, Season 1885-86

Containing accounts of sport in Cheshire, Shropshire, Worcestershire, Staffordshire,

Herefordshire, and Wales

H.F. Mytton, Borderer

Hunting and Sporting Notes in the West Midlands, Season 1885-86
Containing accounts of sport in Cheshire, Shropshire, Worcestershire, Staffordshire, Herefordshire, and Wales

ISBN/EAN: 9783337324483

Printed in Europe, USA, Canada, Australia, Japan

Cover: Foto ©Lupo / pixelio.de

More available books at **www.hansebooks.com**

HUNTING AND SPORTING NOTES

IN THE

WEST MIDLANDS.

SEASON 1885-86.

CONTAINING ACCOUNTS OF
SPORT IN CHESHIRE, SHROPSHIRE, WORCESTERSHIRE, STAFFORDSHIRE,
HEREFORDSHIRE, AND WALES.

BY

"BORDERER."

WITH NUMEROUS

PORTRAITS AND ILLUSTRATIONS

By H. F. MYTTON.

1886.

LONDON:
A. H. BAILY & Co., 15, NICHOLAS LANE.

SHREWSBURY:
"EDDOWES'S JOURNAL" OFFICE, THE SQUARE.

SHREWSBURY: ADNITT & NAUNTON, THE SQUARE.
LUDLOW: A. PARTRIDGE, BROAD STREET
WORCESTER: DEIGHTON & Co., HIGH STREET.

DEDICATED,

BY KIND PERMISSION,

TO

LADY WILLIAMS WYNN.

Bear this in mind throughout the run,
" Faint heart fair lady never won."
Those cravens are thrown out who swerve:
" None but the brave the fair deserve."

INDEX TO ILLUSTRATIONS.

Lady Williams Wynn	Frontispiece
Captain Park Yates	Opposite page ix
Sir Watkin	,, 3
Alfred Thatcher	,, 12
A Wrenbury Greeting	,, 23
Winking his eye at the Colonel from above ...	,, 33
Dislodging the Whittington Fox	,, 34
Sir Vincent Corbet, Bart	37
An Unaccustomed Feat	,, 41
Bolting the Pitchford Fox	,, 43
Death of the Pitchford Fox	,, 44
Two Shropshire Worthies	,, 67
Mr. F. Ames	,, 73
Lord Combermere	,, 95
All for the honour of Shropshire	102

AN INTRODUCTORY CHAPTER TO
HUNTING AND SPORTING NOTES IN
THE WEST MIDLANDS.

NIMROD tells us "That foxhunting suspends the cares of life, whilst the speculations of the racecourse too generally increase them. The one steels the constitution, whilst the anxious cares of the other have a contrary effect. The love of the chase may be said to be screwed into the soul of man by the noble hand of nature, whereas the pursuit of the other is too often the offspring of a passion we should wish to disown. The one enlarges the sympathies, which unite us in a bond of reciprocal kindness and good offices; in the pursuit of the other almost every man is our foe. Lastly, the chase does not usually bring a man into bad company; the modern turf is fast becoming the very manor of the worst."

With this exhilarating opinion before us we are emboldened once again to tempt the fates with a few more hunting notes of the past season. Emboldened, we repeat advisedly, because does it not require some pluck to have to place on record such a season as the one we have endured in 1885-86? Unexampled as one of intermittent frost and snow in its latter part, while its closing November days and early part of December, were equally noticeable for wind, storm, and flood. It needs but to take up to-day's paper (the 15th March), and read the meteorological report, which speaks for itself. It says: "It is now ten weeks since the thermometer in London has registered fifty degrees—during sixty-nine days there have been only five days that it has reached forty-five degrees, on forty-three days it has not reached forty degrees, on twelve days it has not reached thirty-five degrees, and on one day it has remained below freezing point the whole day. At night in a sheltered position, four feet from the ground, it has registered frost on no fewer than forty-nine out of the sixty-nine nights. At Greenwich observatory an instrument placed close to the ground has registered frost on every night except five, and on eleven of these occasions there have been more than ten degrees of frost!" While this has happened in London and its vicinity, how much more has it been felt in other parts of England, especially in the north, and on the western hills. On March 13th, in Wales the snow completely covered the country, and blocked up hedges and gateways. The birds were tame and listless. A woodcock rose out of a ditch by the side of my path and fluttered away, poor fellow, like a half-starved robin. The grouse, too, have had a terrible time of it; hundreds and hundreds have fallen victims to hedge-poppers. I heard of forty brace being hung up in one cellar in a provincial Yorkshire town. Nine hares were picked up dead in a field near Llanarmon —ten miles from Oswestry—last week, and foxes have been making nightly inroads into the town itself in search of food. It seems hardly credible that here we are within six weeks of May Day, skating away as hard as our legs can carry us, with no apparent probability of a change, and all this time Borderer's harp has been hung up on his willow tree; there is no hunting. What a bold man he is even to dream of it, or believe that people will ever want to read anything about such a season as this. The very thought will sicken them, and they will turn with loathing from such "a lost chord." Not at all, my friends. You may not wish the dose repeated. None of us do, but not the less must we retain its record, frail, fleeting, and disappointing though it has been. There are bright spots in it that will always render it memorable. First and foremost it has been the first season of a young generation at Wynnstay. Since last summer's sun glistened on that stately pile its beloved and honoured owner has been taken away from amongst us, and his nephew has been called on to reign in his stead. Last season he had to take much of the active management of the hunt in hand owing to his uncle's failing health, and in doing so, just fresh from Trinity College, Cambridge, he had more than ordinary difficulties to contend with, among which the short comings of the huntsman were not the least. Now, however, all this is altered. Sir Watkin has none of those drawbacks to contend with, which handicapped him last season. He has chosen a huntsman in William Lockey, who coming originally from South Shropshire was not entirely unknown in its Northern parts. He had, it is true, earned no great name as a huntsman in the Worcestershire country, but as an excellent servant, a first-rate horseman, devoted to his hounds, he had few superiors. In this, his first season, I do not hesitate to say he has been a great success. Whatever his shortcomings as a huntsman may have been in the land of fruit and hops, here he has won the hearty approval of a most critical field, in the most decided way. Quiet and yet quick, determined and yet discretionary, he has, in a new country, with everything about it to learn, shown better sport than Sir Watkin's hunt has enjoyed for many a season. Lockey has the fortune, too, to be backed up by one of the keenest Masters, and to be whipped-in by one of the best first whips in the country, in Eli Skinner. With such aids it only needs a pack of hounds improved by careful breeding, drafting, and kennel management, to bring the Wynnstay establishment to a state bordering on perfection. It is worth while to dwell shortly on the past history of Sir Watkin's hunt, to see how the pack has been fostered in the family, and what a grand country it hunts over. The great-great-grandfather of the present Baronet was a noted sportsman in his day, and history tells us how in 1745 he had to quit his native country of Wales for being too closely allied with the Jacobites, and seek shelter with his friend, the then Duke of Beaufort, in Gloucestershire. His second wife was one of the Shakerleys, a good old Cheshire stock, and he died from the effects of a fall, returning from hunting in Sir Robert Cunliffe's park. Curiously enough, this happened according to a presentiment of his wife's, who warned him before starting of her dream. The next inheritor of the title, the son of this last mentioned Sir Watkin, and great-grandfather of the present Baronet, was also a sportsman, and kept a pack of hounds, but his chief delight was the drama. He married a Somerset, and died in 1789. Then came his son, the great Sir Watkin, as he was called in his day. He rode eighteen stone, and knew no fear. Some good stories are extant of him, especially about him and his pad groom, Tom Penn. Nimrod tells an amusing story of how Penn used to rule his master. One day, Sir Watkin and the Hon. Philip Pierrepoint were travelling together, and passed the former's stables in Oxfordshire. "We shall see the horses," said Pierrepoint. "Of course," said Sir Watkin. "Well, Tom," said the Baronet, after alighting from his carriage, "how are the horses?" "The horses are well enough, Sir Watkin, but I am very *hill*." "What ails you?" "Damnationist pain in my side, I ever had in my life." "I should like to see the horses." "You can't, they have been shut up these two hours." The Baronet and his friend had to pursue their journey ungratified! Tom Penn was afterwards killed by a fall out hunting. This Sir Watkin married a Clive, and met his death also from the effects of an accident, being thrown out of a pony carriage in the grounds at Wynnstay. It was during the lifetime of this Sir Watkin, that foxhounds in a regular form were first kept in the Wynnstay country, by Sir Richard Pulestone, of Emral Park. I think we may take it that harriers had been the prevailing delight of former owners of Wynnstay, although, no doubt, they diversified the sport pretty often by hunting foxes when they came across them. Sir Richard Pulestone, however, deserves more than passing mention, as he was one of the pioneers of hunting in Shropshire. In fact, in many ways, he was an accomplished sportsman, and a good judge of hounds, which he hunted himself—a fair horseman, and highly respected throughout a large district. So celebrated was he for hounds, that the Duke of Cleveland bought drafts from him. His "Dromo" blood knew few superiors in those days. The old hound's tomb at Emral bore the inscription:—

Alas, poor Dromo,
Reynard with dread, oft heard his awful name.

Sir Richard bred his own hunters, and Sir Watkin planted several good gorse coverts for him. His chief servants were Jack Bartlett—the quickest whip of his day—Ned Bates, who was his huntsman, when he himself gave up the horn; and last, though not least, Tom Crane, who from a groom, became huntsman of the Fife hounds. He also hunted the Duke of Wellington's pack in the Peninsular War, and was said to have ridden straight among the enemies' bullets sooner than stop his hounds. Sir Richard Pulestone held a sort of moveable feast, hunting the present Albrighton, or as it was then called the Shifnal country, as well as his own. It was at Chillington he made the memorable offer to Ned Bates—" A guinea for old Cæsar." This being the nick-name of an old fox that had beaten his hounds times out of mind, and the reward was never claimed. Curiously enough Sir Richard Pulestone, like the late Mr. Wicksted, finished his hunting career by keeping harriers.

The late Sir Watkin, as we know, was the first owner of

Wynnstay, who from his earliest youth determined upon
keeping a regular pack of foxhounds, after the type of
Sir Richard Pulestone. Mr. Leech on the Carden side of
country, Mr. Mytton and Sir Rowland Hill on the
Shropshire side had kept the ball rolling in succession to
Sir Richard since 1833, but Mytton was too fond of bag-
men, and Mr. Leech hunted after an eccentric fashion.
Sir Watkin was hardly of age before he bought the Carden
pack, and being a soldier in the Household Brigade, he
asked his friend, Mr. Attey, of Lightwood Hall, to take
charge of them, which he did for two seasons. It is a
matter of history, how, when he sold out of the Guards,
he made judicious purchases of hounds, engaged John
Walker from the Fife country (the successor there of
Tom Crane), as his huntsman, and formed in 1845 what
has always since been known as the Wynnstay country.
I am now treading on living history; there are few of us
but have experienced the excellence of Walker, both as a
huntsman and a judge of hounds, and know how long and
faithfully he served a worthy master; and how he was
followed by an equally accomplished huntsman, if not so
great a houndman, in Payne from the Pytchley, and
how his reign nearly equalled that of Walker, while in his
retirement he has survived his Master. Stephen Goodall
took his place for the last two seasons of the late Sir
Watkin's life, and although he came with a great
reputation from Meath, and belonged to a celebrated family
of huntsmen, he failed to win his way at Wynnstay.
No easy matter to follow such men as Walker and Payne.
Goodall is yet young; he has many excellent points in
which he should excel as a huntsman, and Borderer is the
last man to wish to injure one, who, in flying at very high

game has failed. If Goodall will only take to heart the lessons that he has learnt since he left the Meath, we may yet see him a huntsman of no mean repute.

Sir Watkin found the hounds certainly not so even or with so much cry and dash as under Walker's régime but he has made hounds his study from his earliest school boy days, and he whipped-in to his friend Rowland Hunt's Trinity Beagles, so that I do not doubt that he will persevere in the right track here, never forgetting, I trust that nose, tongue and sense must be served, and that without these essentials no pack of hounds in such a varied country as his is, can hope for a general run of good sport. I have heard it said that for several years Sir Watkin's hounds have not been noted for tongue, but this I do know, that when crossed with the Welsh hound, as they were by the late Mr. Robert Luther, so long Master of the United, their tongue and drive are magnificent. I well recollect a big, light-coloured hound called "Wellington" that Walker gave to Luther; he was very deficient in tongue himself, but his blood did wonders with Luther's light bitches, and few, if any of them, were silent. It would be treason, I fear, to advise a dip back into United blood, just by way of trial, and yet I have not the slightest doubt but that the result would be of great benefit to Wynnstay sport. Sir Watkin has opened his Mastership with some wonderfully good sport, as these notes will show. I have not had so many opportunities of sharing in it as could have been wished, and have often been obliged to be indebted to friends for my accounts of runs, and the scraps of sport I have picked up. Nobody is heartier than Borderer, however, in wishing Sir Watkin and Lady Williams Wynn a long unbroken spell of happiness in their

CAPTAIN PARK YATES.

hunting. Theirs is a position unrivalled in the world for friends, supporters, servants, hounds, and foxes.

In Cheshire things have been pretty much in *statu quo* as far as hunting is concerned—here no changes have taken place. Captain Park Yates and Mr. Reginald Corbet still divide the county with great satisfaction to all concerned. The latter has had by no means such a brilliant season as last year, even allowing for frequent stoppages. I am unable to glean as much of the doings of North Cheshire as I should wish, but am inclined to think that sport has been of an average character. The great figure-heads of Cheshire history in this century are Sir Thomas Stanley, Sir H. Mainwaring, and Captain White, anterior to the present divided dynasties, before which Mr. R. Corbet carried on the country as a whole for several seasons. Nimrod, in speaking of Cheshire, most truly describes it when he says: "On the first two days I hunted with the Cheshire I held the fences in perfect contempt; so far from seeing anything like a 'stopper,' I met with nothing that a hunter could not have got over on three legs. On the third day, however, I altered my opinion of them, and was convinced that it requires a hunter to carry a man over Cheshire. I found some strong quick fences with good wide ditches—but this is not all. In the greater part of Cheshire the fence is placed on a very narrow bank, or 'cop,' as it is termed, and strengthened by a very deep ditch. This not only requires a horse to be quick and ready with his legs—as he must spring from the cop when the ditch is from him—but also it requires a horseman to get him over it with safety, when he becomes a little distressed. Temper also in the horse is indispensible here, and provided he have speed, a hunter that can go well over Cheshire, can go well over almost every other country." I could go through a long list of Cheshire worthies, who have made the country famous for its hunting prowess. Since my last notes appeared Lord Rocksavage has entered upon his family estates as Marquis of Cholmondeley, and it is needless to say that both he and the Marchioness are seldom missing where hounds are to be found—and foxes are as thick as blackberries round the Castle, and in the vale surrounding it. Cheshire lies so handy to the great towns, and has such nice hunting quarters at Broxton, Wrenbury, Crewe, Nantwich, Tarporley, and Whitchurch, that there is little wonder at the big fields, which congregate nearly always at their meets. The Masters must often wish that the majority cared more for hunting and less for riding. Indeed, some of them may be said to resemble the late Mr. William Coke, whose fault was that he was *too fast for hounds!*

Of Shropshire I touched very fully in my last season's notes, and here again there are few changes to note, unless indeed the future may be said to have brightened by Mr. Lonsdale's consent to hunt, free of subscription, the South Country, in addition to the North Country, which, a few years ago, was a separate two-day's-a-week country, presided over successfully by Mr. Hulton Harrop. This is a boon all will appreciate, and it will, I trust, lead to complete harmony in the future. Thatcher still carries the horn, but we have much missed Harry Beavan as first whip. It is satisfactory, however, to hear that he has made such a promising début as a huntsman in the South Staffordshire country. Foxes have been exceedingly plentiful (as indeed they are everywhere this season), but not particularly straight-necked—the best gallops have been rings. The South Country has come out well, especially Pitchford, where Colonel Cotes has been resident, instead of having his horses at Whitchurch, and has shown lots of foxes, and good ones. Hardwick Gorse has never failed. Shawbury and the Lea have been as usual prolific, and so have Preston Gubbalds and Leaton. Ercall has been unlucky; Twemlows not so good as last season; Losford has yielded one brilliant gallop; Battlefield is better than last year; Holly Coppice and Sundorne have scarcely been asked a question since the season began; Preston Springs and Acton Reynald have yielded good runs, and so has Loppington one run—while Coton has not been tenantless. Peplow, Chetwynd and the Drayton side are nothing to boast of, while Withington Wood, one of the best in the hunt, has not had a hound in it this season! The Master is about to change his quarters from Gredington to Shavington, which will place him a trifle nearer his kennels. Borderer trusts that the bad scent, which hung about the general election time, will not recur, and that the future of Shropshire will bear favourable comparison with the past —we cannot see how the most devoted Conservative could better the cause of foxhunting by declining to support the present régime.

In the Albrighton Country I have had fewer opportunities of enjoying myself than last year, but I fear that, except in November, I have not been a great loser, as Sir Thomas and Lady Boughey have not had a more trying season during their long apprenticeship in the country, and this, too, from no fault but the utter perversity of our climate, which in a plough country like this, is fatal to scent. Both

Scott and Will Jones, the huntsman, and first whip, are excellent servants, and slaves to sport; the hounds are first-rate, and all mean business, so that I cannot but condole with them over the circumstances over which they have no control.

North Staffordshire is much in the same state as the Albrighton, except, perhaps, that Dickens is not quite so keen as he used to be. I have heard of his staying at home on days, that to us, appeared warrantable hunting ones—such as the Shropshire Atcham Bridge Friday, when the ground rode softly enough, in all conscience. Still, Dickens knows his business, and can hunt a fox against most men. I wish this vile long frost had not upset Borderer's calculations of having a few days with them.

The Ludlow do not crow with their whilom vigour. There have been very few of those long point to point runs that so cheered and enlivened them last season. Radnorshire has not once been touched upon; although the North Hereford about Docklow and Marston Firs has been paid a visit—and the Worcestershire at Clifton-on-Teme. In truth, there is a great grief here, because their pleasant paths for the last twenty years have been rudely interrupted, and they have awakened to the fact that Mr. Wicksted and they are to part, not wholly, but as their Master. I can scarcely trust myself to speak on this matter, where old associations and friendships are so nearly concerned. There was a flicker of hope that the chord would not be broken, and yet it has gone, and Sir William Curtis of Caynham Court is now elected the future Master of the destinies of the Ludlow.

The history of the Ludlow country is interesting, and

has not been told for many years. Mr. Richard Dansey of Easton Court, my great-grandfather, may be said to have been its first master, though he hunted the Herefordshire side of the county more than in Shropshire, while Mr. Childe, of Kinlet, took the Cleobury and Clee Hill side. Mr. Adams came next, and lived at Ludlow, with his coadjutor, Mr. Robert Price of Bitterley, a noted sportsman of his day, the father of Colonel R. H. Price, Master of the Radnorshire and West Hereford Hounds. The picture of old Adams cheering on his hounds, adorns many a South Shropshire wall. Mr. Dansey was a great friend of Lord Forester, and of Nimrod, and the latter speaks in very high terms of him as a sportsman—his voice was so musical, and his style of encouraging his hounds was so like Musters. A good story is told of his having dismounted one day to alter his girths or saddle, just as the hounds were finding their fox, and being unable to mount very quickly, he, at last, seized a favourable opportunity, and got well back into his saddle. A lamentable disaster however occurred—crack went his braces. "There, by Jove," said he to himself, "there's a pretty job—I have only taken to wear braces six weeks, and I'll bet a guinea I lose my breeches before we kill this fox." Mr. Dansey's son also hunted part of the Ludlow country, and afterwards became Master of the Oakley. Mr. Adams was celebrated for having a huntsman that rode a mule, and had the best hands on him that you could conceive. After Adams and the second Mr. Dansey, came Mr. Stubbs of the Whetmore—who, aided by his son Orlando, a capital performer in the pigskin, and on old Gideaway, Moorcock, and others farmed the local cups—hunted these hounds for a long period, showing capital sport. Orlando Stubbs afterwards took the the Albrighton country, and died there. He was a dashing huntsman in his best day, something of the style of Jem Hills, and never dwelt over bad scenting ploughs. Lord Giffard came here for a season or two from Herefordshire, and then Mr. W. H. Sitwell, of Ferney Hall took them, and to him the country owes a great deal. The hounds were judiciously drafted and improved, and although in Nichol he had hardly a heaven born huntsman, he showed what a thoroughly disinterested and hearty country gentleman can do, to keep a hunt together for the enjoyment of all. His reign lasted ten seasons, when, in 1863, he was succeeded by Major Murray, a local man, a good horseman, fond of a gallop between the flags, and riding nice horses; but the cares of office soon began to sit heavily upon him, and he made way for Mr. C. W. Wicksted in 1866, whose father had left Cheshire and North Staffordshire for the rougher locality of Shakenhurst in Worcestershire, where he amused himself with about the most perfect little pack of harriers in Europe. Charles junior had inherited the same fondness for hounds as his father, and what was more to the purpose, was an equally fine judge of their best points. He had, when he became Master of the Ludlow, very good ground to work upon, as Mr. Sitwell had spared no expense in getting drafts from Belvoir, Sir Watkin's, and the Berkeley—and with George Hills as huntsman, he soon made the sport a speciality. In 1869, George Hills went to the Herefordshire, and Mr. Wicksted took the horn with William Lockey, promoted from whip to kennel huntsman and first whip. This happy union lasted till 1879, when Lockey went as huntsman to Captain Ames in Worcestershire, and J. Overton took his place with the Ludlow. Since then there have been frequent changes in the kennels, until at the beginning of last season the Master once more resigned the horn to Johnson, who holds the place still, and I believe goes on with Sir William Curtis, in the same capacity. So great and adept at kennel management and hound lore is Mr. Wicksted, that he has compiled a regular hound stud book, which shows the descent of his present pack from 1853, when Mr. Sitwell first became Master, and he has most cleverly contrived to trace his own blood throughout more than thirty years of management. The Ludlow is such a wide Country, running into four Counties, and its woodlands are so strong that it requires immense energy and love of hunting for a man to succeed in it. It requires, too, a pack of hounds full of tongue and drive to get foxes away from their strongholds, and this has been the chief difficulty that all Masters of this Country have had to contend with since Borderer's earliest hunting days. Wicksted taking the cue from his father has always been a stickler for blood—a hound cannot be too high-bred for him—unmindful, I venture often to think, that it is not the strong point of these high-bred ones to struggle through difficulties, speaking frequently and carrying a head through coverts of from one-hundred to a thousand acres; consequently he has suffered from slackness in his pack, when the scent has not served, and long tiring days have brought him little or no blood. We none of us like to acknowledge our neighbours to be better than ourselves, nor are they, altogether, in this instance, and yet I believe that the crossed blood of the United is better suited to the Ludlow Country than the beautiful pack that hunts it. " Self-willed devils," I fancy I hear some good man say. " How can Borderer be such a fool." Well granted even that, nevertheless more sport and finer straightaway runs will be had with these 'strong-willed,' dashing, low scented, persevering devils over rough and smooth ground, taken together, than with any other kind of hound you can mention.

> " . . . . Never did I hear
> Such gallant chiding ; for besides the groves,
> The skies, the fountains, every region near
> Seem all one mutual cry ;
> I never heard so musical a discord, such sweet thunder."

All that is required with such a pack as the United is good kennel management. By this I mean keeping the pack under proper control, and teaching them a due respect, and perfect obedience to their huntsman. They then become the easiest managed hounds in the world, still retaining sufficient self-reliance to carry them through difficulties, which a high-bred foxhound would scorn to submit to without the cheering voice of his huntsman. Such are the United now under the management of Old Alec, once with the Wheatland, and still mastered by Mr. John Harris, the most worthy yeoman of the Montgomeryshire border, a man, who beyond all others deserves the appreciation in which he is held far and wide in his own country. The sport shown by the United this year has been wonderful. The average of foxes said to have been killed after good runs is something extraordinary, but I am afraid to repeat it from hearsay. And if any of my readers, who are hound lovers, will take the trouble to go and have a look over this pack on the flags, and in their work, I will answer for it they will return with new ideas of what hounds like these are capable of, and if not convinced that all is not quite as it should be with them, at least they will admit that they are very wonderful animals. Sir William Curtis has yet his spurs to win, but I have confidence that with health and vigour he will both succeed in doing this, and wearing them. He gives up a most perfect pack of beagles, his success with which are a most hopeful sign for him as an M.F.H.

The Wheatland have had a most chequered career for many seasons, and now Captain Summers after only one season's mastership, I hear, is going to retire. The disappointment is all the worse as it was thought when he took them, that the arrangement would have been a permanent one. Coming from Pembrokeshire he had been well schooled for his work, and brought with him a keenness and desire to excel, which I thought augured well for himself and the country. One thing he has undoubtedly done even in his short tenure of office. He has improved the pack. They are most workmanlike, have a rare lot of tongue, and hunt together like a pack of beagles. They are admirably suited to the country, which in some of its attributes is the best in Shropshire, and there is nothing I should like better, if Providence so ordained it, than to throw in my lot with the Wheatland. Such a fine wild, scenting country, not cut up by railways, nor worried by monster fields—where every man is a sportsman, and there are few drags to the coach. Old Forester, of Willey, once said of the Wheatland in answer to a question whether he approved of the men there, "Very much, sir," said he. "I did not see one d—d fellow in white top boots among the whole field; depend upon it they are sportsmen."

In Herefordshire things I rejoice to say continue with little alteration. Captain Lutwyche has consented to continue his mastership, which, for the last few years has been in commission almost annually, much to the damage of its prestige. His sport this season, especially since Christmas, has been above the average, Sutton Walls and the Bodenham country being the scenes of good runs. It is curious to notice how seldom scent lies in this country until after Christmas. I have noticed it for years past, and the foxes seem aware of it also, for they go straighter. Captain Freke Lewis and Mr. Helme have, as joint masters, in the South, changed places. The latter now takes the horn, and the former the field management. How the change will answer next season will prove. They both have their hearts in the work, and have been judiciously crossing their hounds with the Llangibby.

Colonel Price in West Hereford and Radnorshire is, like Mr. Wicksted in the Ludlow county, the figurehead of the ship, although they differ in their appreciation of Welsh blood. Colonel Price, it is true, found the blood to his hand when he came from the Southdown country, and was not at first so much in love with it as experience has since taught him to be—still the result has been a wonderful and unbroken success. Colonel Price still hunts them himself, and shows sport of which any huntsman need be proud. The pack to look at is unique. More like the United perhaps than any other, but stronger in the backs, and lower on the legs, and their handiness as well as cleverness are remarkable. Some tremendous runs were enjoyed this season, especially in the early part of it. One run from Rhydspence, close to Whitney, straight to

Glasewm, and killing him there, within a few miles of Builth, speaks for itself. It could not have been much less than twenty miles. Another from the big woods near Presteign to the Craigie rocks, and back across the Vale of Radnor to Burvah, covers a fair lot of ground. The West Hereford country has also done well. A fox from close to Kinnersley took them to Lady Lift and Robin Hood's Butt, and on to Kings' Pyon, where he got on some buildings and managed to dodge them. He was found dead the next morning, two fields further on, however, from over exertion. The field were lost (including the master) in Lady Lift. Would any hounds without a Welsh cross have gone entirely through this immense woodland unaided, and for miles beyond? Nobody reached them until long after the run was over.

Mr. Reginald Herbert takes the Monmouthshire, I hear, in succession to Captain Hanbury Williams.

I have not yet touched on the Worcestershire, although they certainly ought not to be passed by in silence. One day that I have had with them this season at the Red Lion, Holt, has been by some means omitted from my notes. It was not a distinguished day, and yet it is worthy of mention, and shall be added here.

"On Wednesday, the 11th, I stumbled upon the Worcestershire at the Red Lion, Holt. Denton, the new huntsman, had a pretty and workmanlike pack of bitches, and the turn-out was all that it should be. I was amused at the unusual incident of a lady riding up to the meet laden with sandwiches or prog of some kind, which she presented to the huntsman and whips. So big were the parcels that they filled even their capacious pockets. The field dropped in to the tune of fifty or sixty, and away we went to Ockeridge Wood, a big hundred-acre covert, very often the abode of a good fox. To-day we took up a position in the middle ride, and to only a few did the sound of a find come at the top corner, and even these did not realize the fact that hounds were away until the sound waxed fainter each moment. An unfortunate scrimmage occurring at the moment, owing to two horses becoming oddly entangled in the reins of the other, made matters worse, and we trust Mr. Watson, of Waresley, was none the worse for his encounter with mother earth. Meanwhile hounds had gone away almost alone over a good line towards Martley, and only one of the field, good between the flags, had caught them. It was an amusing stampede, which a check close to Martley Church put straight, and with united forces, and at a slower pace, we crossed the main road close to the workhouse, and journeyed over the hill until we faced the river Teme below Shelsley. Here he dropped down as if to cross, and ran the meadows, leaving Ankerdine Wood and hill on his left, until within a mile of Knightsford Bridge, when he crossed, and the remaining field had to bustle on to the bridge, if they intended to see them again. Personally, Borderer was doing a bird's-eye view of the fun from the hill. Hounds now ran into the Ledbury country at Whitbourne alone, and then turned up the other bank of the river to Clifton-on-Teme. The huntsman picked them up, and viewed his fox dead beat close to them, I heard, but failed to bring him to hand, so that after a long run of more than three hours, he lives to fight again. Hounds probably changed near Ankerdyne, but, be this as it may, it was a sporting day, and showed me that the Worcestershire are in good form, and that Denton knows his business. He was quiet and patient, with plenty of nerve and determination when required. During Mr. Ames' mastership the Worcestershire have done well. Great care has been taken in rearing the hounds and keeping together a pack worthy of the sporting shire, where farmers support foxhunting almost to a man. It is now fourteen years since Worcestershire was divided into two countries. The west side under the Earl of Coventry, being called the Croome. From the day that he left college, some thirty years ago, Lord Coventry has devoted himself to hunting in his own county. Racing for a short time claimed him as its devotee, but his old love never really was put aside. As a huntsman he was quick and decisive. As a horseman bold and judgmatical. As a master of hounds, good-natured and popular. While as a judge of horse or hound he yields to no superior. Lord Coventry gave up the Croome country to Mr. Lort Philips three seasons ago, and he in turn yielded up authority to Mr. Walter Greene, from Suffolk, two seasons back, and the latter has won his way well, as he deserves to do. Mr. Lort Philips has taken the North Warwickshire, where he appears more at home. There are several old masters of the Worcestershire living. Lord Hindlip, when plain Mr. Allsopp, was master for several seasons, and before him Mr. John Russell Cookes was master—a capital sportsman, always breeding and riding good horses, a cheery man in every relation of life. There is a sad page in the history of masters of the Worcestershire, as the late Mr. Parker, a well-known old sportsman of the county, ended his days, I believe in poverty. He was a great friend of Nimrod's, who thus speaks of him; "This I can say of Mr. Parker that, next to Mr. Charles Boultbee, I consider him the best man on a bad hunter—indeed no hunter at all—that I ever saw. The seat and hand of Mr. Parker appeared to be perfect as to giving assistance to his horse over a deep country like Worcestershire; and for nerve I need not go beyond the fact of my seeing him ride an old groggy horse over a good gate in a very hard frost." Another old sportsman alluded to by the same author, as a compeer of Mr. Parker's, was Mr. John Price, of Ryall, not only a breeder of horses and an accomplished horseman, but a great Herefordshire cattle breeder—he actually refused two thousand guineas (a rattling price in those days), for the pick of ten of his best cows, bar one! He knew how to sell his horses, for he sold two to the then Lord Deerhurst for five hundred guineas each—one of which, that he called " Judgment," had all the best of a big run in the Grafton country with him for a pilot. Speaking of that heavy side of the country, from Pershore and Droitwich to Redditch, adjoining Warwickshire, which is undoubtedly the best scenting, and the pick of Worcestershire in a hunting point of view, the present agricultural depression has materially added to its attractions—an immense extent of country formerly under plough has been allowed to go untilled, and rough pasture now abounds, where formerly wheat grew. The old Hanbury Forest bids fair to reassert itself, and scrubby blackthorn bushes are already springing up all over the fields, making it a fine wild country, with fences that require a hunter to negotiate. I am glad to say that Worcestershire under Mr. Ames, still brings out some good riders to hounds, and that there is some young blood springing up of the never-to-be-denied stamp, which bids fair to keep alive the sterling spirit of horsemanship for which the fruit and hop shire has been so long celebrated.

The following will, I believe, prove to be a correct

chronological table of Worcestershire masterships and their huntsmen since 1830 :—

YEAR.	MASTERS.	HUNTSMEN.
1830 to 1836	Mr. Parker	Himself.
1837 to 1845	Captain Chandler	Carter and Grant.
1846	A Committee, Hon. Dudley Ward, chairman	T. Mathews.
1847 to 1849	J. R. Cookes, Esq	T. Mathews & Will Stansby in 1848.
1850 to 1854	Major Clowes	Do.
1855 to 1856	J. R. Cookes, Esq	John Ward.
1857 to 1864	Major Clowes. J. R. Cookes, Esq. } Jointly	W. Mawe.
1865	H. F. Vernon, Esq	Do.
1866 to 1869	H. F. Vernon, Esq H. Allsopp, Esq } Jointly	Do. George Orvis in 1868.
1870 to 1871	The Marquis of Queensbury.	Himself.
In 1872 the Country was divided to 1873	The Earl of Coventry took the Croome, and H. Allsopp, Esq. the Worcestershire	Thos. Carr.
1874 to 1876	F. Ames, Esq	Do.
1877 to 1879	C. Morrell, Esq	Himself.
1880 to 1886	F. Ames, Esq	Will. Lockey, Charles Denton in 1885.

The Ledbury and Cotswold also come into the West Midland District, but in such a chequered season it was impossible to get round them. Their sport, I fear, has not been quite up to the mark. No country could have been harder hit than the Cotswold with the intermittent frost, snow, hail, and wind, with which it has been favoured, and I hope that Mr. Hicks-Beach, the new Master, will not be discouraged, but persevere, and succeed.

Nothing but the same excuse prevented me paying my usual trip into Yorkshire, and diversifying these notes with a whisper of their doings. I am delighted to be able to state, from a friendly authority of the best description, that that pillar of hunting and all that appertains to it, Mr. George Lane Fox, is slowly but surely recovering from his serious illness, and with returning Spring, he trusts to rise once more equal to the occasion of responding to the toast, "The Bramham and its twenty-five couple."

There are many other things that may have been said about fox-hunting as a whole, and the West Midlands in particular, which have been left unsaid, in this second series of my notes for the past year, but the circumstances under which they have been written have had a depressing effect on their author, and were it not that his young and rising artist, Mr. H. F. Mytton, had spurred him on by his spirited sketches and promise of assistance, and that Sir Watkin and Lady Williams Wynn and other good sportsmen had put not only their portraits at his behest, but also their good wishes, he would fain not have attempted it. To wait, however, for a more convenient season that may never come, is not a foxhunter's motto. We always try to take things as they come, and come what may, we accept the country over which our fox chooses to take us—only delighting to ride straight, give hounds room, and not interfere with other people—a quick eye, steady nerve, soft hand, strong grip, and good temper, carry a man over many troubles, and, I trust, will continue to do so long after the notes of the season 1885-86 have passed into oblivion.

HUNTING AND SPORTING NOTES
IN
THE WEST MIDLANDS.

FIRST WEEK, October 26th to 31st.

How soon November slips round again, and how as each year succeeds another we look forward more or less keenly to the opening hunting season. In fulfilment of my promise to give the readers of *Eddowes's* once again a few notes of sport in Shropshire, I gladly take up my pen—first of all thanking the many good friends who have purchased my sporting notes of 1884 and 1885, and expressed kindly criticisms upon them. I can answer for my young artist's ability to improve his handicraft, but, perhaps, with Borderer the reverse is the case, for these bad times and other hard work will keep him more out of the field than his inclinations would have him do. This season opens very differently to last year, for instead of having a very dry autumn we have lately been blessed with a good steady downpour, which has filled our rivers, brooks, ditches, and furrows, laid low the leaves, and made the opening days this week hopeful in every way of scent and sport. Foxes undoubtedly have bred more freely than usual, as there is hardly a pack in the United Kingdom that does not say that foxes are plentiful, so that hounds have tasted plenty of blood. Horses have not suffered from the hard ground, and everything is ready for a good beginning. With the Wynnstay hunt, as your readers are all aware, a change has come over the scene, owing to the late Sir Watkin's death—an event that all sportsmen, of whatever type, most deeply deplored, because they felt that they had thus lost the head and front of hunting in the county. A man, who, for more than forty years, had done everything that money, influence, tact, and experience could do to make their pleasures of the hunting second to none in the United Kingdom. Sir Watkin, however, still lives in his successor, and building, as the present Sir Watkin will do, on the foundations and example set him so splendidly, I have not the slightest doubt that, if all goes well with him, he will have a still greater chronicle of success to hand on, let us hope, to a long line of heirs.

With a stable full of nice horses, an improved pack of hounds, a keen heart, a new huntsman, and all the country at his back, what can he wish for more, in a sporting sense, in this sublunary world! William Lockey, his new huntsman, I have known so many years that I am shy of saying too much of him, for fear it should be considered mere fulsome praise. No man ever won his spurs so thoroughly as he did while in the Ludlow country—as a whip he was certainly the best I ever saw there, while in kennel management he had a master, who delighted to teach him everything. When he went into Worcestershire the Ludlow men grieved terribly. It took him some time to shake off the whip and become the huntsman—a place in which very few men have succeeded in Worcestershire. The truth to tell, it is essentially a blind and difficult country, inhabited by fast pushing men. It carries a poor scent and its foxes are short-running, torturous beggars, as a rule. The hedges are so high and uncut, and there is so much hedgerow timber, that a huntsman has a poor chance of getting forward, and kills few foxes. With all this, Lockey has left many staunch friends in Worcestershire, and will, I am sure, make many fresh ones in Shropshire. He has temper,

Sir Watkin Williams Wynn, Bart.

discretion, perseverance and pluck—four rare good attributes in any man, be he huntsman, or Prime Minister.

The many gallops that already have been wafted on the wind to me have been delightful. Ash has afforded one, so has the Nesscliffe country, and the Woodhouse, near Rednal, an extraordinarily fine run over a line second to none in Shropshire, leaving Halston on his left, straight to Petton, a little beyond which they fairly nailed him in the open, a good eight mile point of superb galloping. No wonder that all the stables in Whitchurch are taken, and that orders for breeches and boots in North Shropshire exceed previous records. Mr. Lonsdale has only changed his whips, Harry Beavan having gone as huntsman to Mr. Foster in South Staffordshire. I fear we shall miss him, as the new men, I hear, do not shake into their places quite so well, or seem able to get over the country so quickly as Harry used to do. Every allowance should be made, however, because the country is strange to them. Thatcher brings a beautiful pack into the field, and has had a good cub-hunting. Among several good mornings, one from Leaton Knolls, and another from Condover must not be forgotten, while from Walford last week they had two very good gallops that pleased everybody. Young Thatcher takes his place in the field for the first time as second horseman, and will, I have little doubt, soon earn promotion, for he is a smart boy.

Of the Albrighton, all I hear is most cheering, and there cannot be a doubt that the season thus far suits the country. You will hear of good sport here. I failed to get to the Stretton Meet, or should have spoken more in the present tense.

Mr. Summers, in the Wheatland Country, I have failed to hear much about as yet, but your pages shall bear record of their doings ere long, if Borderer's friend is faithful to his promise.

The Ludlow, too, have not telephoned me as yet any news of importance. Scent before the rain was insufficient for their purpose, although foxes there are in plenty. Since then Johnson has been warming to his work considerably. Saturday was a drenching day for the usual

Ferney Hall opening Meet. The United are by all accounts in good form, and shall not be forgotten hereafter.

Shrewsbury Races will engross attention this week, and intending visitors to them will be struck with the new broom that has been at work there The Racecourse Company have indeed not been idle, and I think it will be universally admitted that their expenditure has been judicious. To prophesy is dangerous, and yet I cannot but prognosticate success, so ample are the capabilities of the ground, and so willing are its new proprietors to develop them.

SECOND WEEK, NOVEMBER 2ND TO 7TH.

Not all the foresight or new brooms can ensure fine days in November, and so the directors and managers of Shrewsbury Racecourse Company had to contend with alternate sunshine and storm of no ordinary kind on Thursday. It was pitiable to see the poor little jockey boys at the post for the Bradford Nursery in a blinding hailstorm. The ladies of Shropshire, however, showed splendid pluck, for they were there, notwithstanding the elements; and if youth, beauty, birth, and munificence were not well represented on the Stewards' Stand Borderer's judgment must have been greatly at fault. Hospitality, too, seemed boundless; for no less than 250 dined at one table, in relays. The officers of the Shropshire Regiment came out right loyally, and so did Leaton, Berwick, Chirk Castle, and Acton Reynald. Unfortunately, Thursday's Steeplechase did not fill, and so the new course had to wait another day before being christened. Boundary, Mirth, Cohort, and Caradoc were names appropriate and of good omen among Thursday's winners; while, on Friday, one of our oldest and best patrons of sport in all its branches, the Duke of Beaufort, won the Cup with the Eastern Emperor, in a grandly run race. Many a knowing one's head shook ominously when Eastern Emperor was not started for the Shropshire Handicap, and kept for the Cup instead, because two miles was considered beyond his compass.

In a fast run race he appeared, a mile from home, to be almost out of the race, and little Martin did not begin to join the front rank until they came into the straight, where some of the leaders ran wide, and with a splendid rush, he brought him up on the inside, and settled the question of his stamina there and then. A real Shropshire cheer greeted his return to the paddock. I hope next season to see the Shrewsbury Cup made worth £500, for there is not a finer long distance handicap run during the year than this, following the Cesarewitch. Two grand looking horses carried off the Steeplechase, in Red Hussar and Old Joe, and, perhaps, both are much nearer the top of the tree in their line of business than many people suppose. Œnone made a good fight for the Hunt Cup, when she got on to the course at the finish, not having been able to make up her ground in the plough, which told its tale on Chancellor also.

I shall hope to see the New Steeplechase Course in great vogue in the first week in April, when there will be stakes for local horses as well as for the best of every class. It is cheering to know that the receipts of the meeting more than came up to previous expectations, taking into consideration that the free list was a large one. Several important improvements are on the tapis, and will, I trust, be carried out forthwith.

And now let us get back to the hunting. Sir Watkin had a rambling, jumping, tumbling, and bathing day, on Wednesday, when his meet was Whitchurch racecourse. Sandford never fails them, and to-day's fox (or foxes) chose a new line to his predecessors of last season, as he broke by the cottage and over the Market Drayton road for Hawkstone. Here an eager field encountered probably the biggest and blindest fences in the county, to say nothing of peaty meadows, until he crossed the Losford brook, and hid himself in Losford covert, where the Shropshire luckily had done plenty of work two days before; forced from here, he popped down over the brook below Bletchly, where it takes some jumping (the exact scene of my artist's picture of last season, only the reverse way.) Bank full now, it seemed to invite victims, who loathingly adapted themselves to circumstances, a gallant colonel finding himself and horse on opposite sides of this charming obstacle. It cost him another wetting to regain his quad, and some hard riding to catch the hounds, which had gone to Styche, and then over the brook for Little Drayton, describing a circle by Tern Hill, towards Losford again, with more brook jumping towards Styche again, where eventually he went to ground at the end of two hours and forty minutes. Altogether, Losford brook was crossed six times, and I leave my readers to judge how many immersions there were of those who declined to look for a bridge—generally an average of one in six.

While all this was being enacted on the Cheshire side, the Shropshire were working away in the morning at Lythwood, with a very bad fox that declined to show sport, and was killed close to the Hall. A brace in Bomere (this is an improvement on last season) were headed at starting, and declined to trust themselves in the open afterwards. From Pitchford, in the evening, a fox went away to Eaton Mascott, disturbing another en route from Golding plantation, so that foxes hereabouts are not wanting, and some fun must be in store for us, if earth stopping is attended to.

The Albrighton, I should have said, found themselves on Tuesday at four p.m., at Maer Hills, in the centre of the North Stafford County, thirty miles from their kennels, having started from Offley Grove in the morning. Had not three-and-a-half couple slipped away in front of the other this would have been a grand run. Sir Thomas Boughey has, I hear, promised to come into his Newport country on a Saturday—this will be some recompense to the Shrewsburyites for the loss of a Whitchurch Saturday.

The United on Friday, from Strefford's Bridge, enjoyed the, to them, unusual prospect of finding a brace in Felhampton square covert near the railway, not more than fifteen acres in extent, and running there for two hours without cessation, neither fox breaking and both saving their lives. Another of this brilliant litter declined even to get out of the way of the mail train last week while eating a rabbit, and consequently the aforesaid mail train accomplished more than old Alec could, for it there and then cut off all four pads and his brush, and there lay his carcase the next morning with the partly-devoured rabbit by his side! Fact, not fiction, this, as the stationmaster at Craven Arms will vouch, if desired. In the evening these hounds had a rattling gallop to ground in Millichope Park.

On Saturday the vicious elements had expended their wrath, and as nice a hunting morning opened for the meet of the Shropshire, at Berwick Hall, as could possibly have been desired. A good field availed themselves of the opportunity, and Mr. Watson gave a warm welcome to all. The big wood failed to hold a fox, and also the Pool Covert, but no sooner had the hounds been thrown into a snug gorse, of which I forget the name, than there was a holloa back. In the result the hounds refused to own a line, and Hencote Pool was requisitioned. Here a fox was on his legs instantly, and, after a few minutes of musical pressure, broke towards the Wem Road, and then swung round by Hencote Farm to the rifle range, but scent came to an end here and he had probably doubled on the railway. Thatcher hit him off near his starting place, and thence by a devious uncertain route he took us to Bircheymoor, the field following in very listless straggling order. From here they ran smartly to Albrighton Hall, where he was dodging about the garden evidently beaten, when Thatcher became enamoured of a holla the Gubbalds way, and, of course, fresh foxes were on foot here. One at last got away, after being headed by a hunting carriage and pair, and, turning away from Pimhill, took us what would have been a good line if it had had the important element of straightness about it, till we found ourselves, after many turnings, near Leaton Station, then back again among houses, gardens and small inclosures, with the accompanying shouts of many strong lungs that rendered hunting a farce and a delusion; towards Pimhill, which he eventually reached despite the fact that a fresh fox appeared on the scene from a little coppice en route. Here he gave up the ghost and was eaten, much to my relief, as he was anything but a straight-necked one. It was now 3-30 p.m., and without a second horse it seemed cruel to go on to Hardwicke, with the almost certain contingency of finding another fox. The country rode very heavy and strange to say with a bad scent. I daresay Borderer will be scolded for finding fault, but, oh! if our Shropshire field would only restrain their ardour, especially along the roads, when hounds are not running in front of them, and also their voices when they view foxes in the open, when hounds are close at hand, how much they would contribute to sport.

THIRD WEEK, November 9th to 14th.

Events that have interested sporting men and women have come upon us thickly this last week, and helped to check the political mania so rife amongst us.

A link with the past generation has been broken. The familiar form of Mrs. Clement Hill has passed away from amongst us. The daughter of Mr. John Mytton, of Halston, better known as "Jack Mytton," Mrs. Clement Hill inherited, in a marked degree, his nerve and sporting tastes. In the heyday of her life few could cross a country or enjoy sport as she could, and she entered into it with a gusto seldom seen in her sex now-a-days. When no longer able to ride she rarely missed a meet on wheels with the Cheshire, Sir Watkin, or the Shropshire, that came within a ten mile radius of Whitchurch, and her familiar figure has been depicted most effectively in Borderer's Sporting Notes of 1884-85, by her nephew. In marrying into the Hill family she added another connection between the three great families, with which sport in Shropshire will always be connected—the Corbets, Hills, and Myttons.

Turning to a pleasanter subject I find the week's calendar chronicles the marriage of Miss Biddulph, of Chirk Castle, with Mr. H. T. Barclay. Happy in every sense is this sporting match, and we trust that Shropshire and Cheshire pastures will occasionally tempt these young people to forsake Leicestershire, just to show us how our easier, and yet more varied country can be got over in good form. I hear the presents were simply magnificent, and Borderer's blessings should be included.

Of hunting the week has been full, and scent fair, but nothing really good has reached me from near home.

On Monday, Sir Watkin at Baschurch went Boreatton way, but I hear no brag of the business done. On Tuesday Mr. R. Corbet drew his usually large and eager cavalcade to Wrenbury Station, and gave them an enjoyable day, in which all could have a cut in, as the foxes took the open well, but did not run straight. Wrenbury Mosses produced two rings with separate foxes, the first a twenty minutes in the direction of Baddiley, and the second over a like line, only not such a big circuit. In both runs the foxes ran home, and saved themselves. In the afternoon from Marley Moss, they ran smartly past Marbury to Norbury Common, then towards Cholmondeley, and back to Norbury stick covert to ground, in about an hour, which wound up the day well.

On Wednesday, the Shropshire turned out in capital style, at Acton Reynald, where it is needless to say that Sir Vincent was delighted to hold out a foxhunter's hand to all. The first fox betook himself at once to Grinshill, and popped himself into a rabbit hole. Number two from Moreton Corbet wood, was a better sort, for he meant business, leaving Shawbury village on his left, passed through Matthew's coppice and Shawbury Heath to Sir Vincent's gorse, and hotly pursued, gave them a taste of grass, and hairy fences up to the drain at Hadnal village, which ended several bursts last season, and is evidently well-known by most of the foxes hereabouts. If Mr. Ward would put a grating on it, hunting men would be grateful. What the evening produced Borderer knows not. Nor does he say anything about Thursday, except that the dancing dames and damsels of the county drew their annual concourse of hunt uniforms together in the Music Hall, and went in for thorough enjoyment throughout the night. The usual crowd was wanting owing chiefly to improved arrangements amplifying the room. I believe that the Peris of the evening were a peeress, who divides the favour of her residence between Worcestershire and Shropshire, and a lady commoner, whose husband holds, or did hold, a military post amongst us.

To Atcham Bridge went an unusually gay cavalcade on Friday morning, and the elements were as propitious as they had been the reverse last season on the same occasion. It is many years since so many carriages have graced this beautiful meet, and at least a couple of hundred horsemen comprised the field. Several new pinks found it a most fitting occasion to be aired, and well might the master be congratulated on the soul inspiring scene, as a manifesto in favour of foxhunting. The business of the day began with a vain search through Attingham Park and withy beds. Ravenshaw gorse, splendidly situated for a gallop, put life into the day's proceedings. Its fox went away boldly for the Wrekin, and for three or four fields bold hearts grew bolder, and the timid ones looked ominously forward to the big hill a few miles ahead. Before, however, reaching the Wellington Road, the fox turned left-handed, and crossed the railway down to the River Tern. Here came visions of swimming or turning, which were not put to the test, for the adversary's heart was weak, and he declined a crossing, retracting his steps over the railway, only to yield up his brush near the point of departure, at Duncote; a ring full of promise at first ending too soon. A trot towards Longner followed, and Thatcher, taking the withy bed near the meet en route, unexpectedly revealed number two, that went off for Longner House, unearthing a large luncheon party as the hounds and field dashed past the windows. Hugging the river to Preston Boats, and, on opposite Belvidere, he turned across the railway and Uffington farm. Up to Haughmond Hill, a very pretty gallop, with some jumping, sufficient to make the Atcham day an equal to its predecessors. Here fresh foxes were going, and scent got worse.

Saturday, the 14th, the Albrighton met at Wilbrighton, but beyond ringing the changes about Aqualate, and then getting away towards Wood Eaton, not much fun resulted, I hear.

Very good accounts reach me of sport in West

Herefordshire. Colonel Price had a splendid run from Almeley, on Monday, the 9th. Finding in Foster's Wood, close to the meet, hounds ran across the railway to Elsdon, nearly to Penrhos, then left-handed to Bollingham and Queesmoor, nearly to Cwmma Moor. Skirting this, he crossed the Apostle's Lane, down to the Arrow, and past Huntingdon nearly to Gladestry, then to the right over Hargest Ridge nearly to Kington. Once more swinging round the hill, this splendid fox managed to crawl into an earth in Worzel with the pack at his brush and saved his life. The pace was good all the way, and their run could not have been less than fifteen miles. A very good day I hear also resulted on Friday from Huntingdon, of which I have not space to speak.

The Welshpool stag hunt came off a few days back—a sporting feast, which seems to partake very much of the old defunct Epping Hunt. Lord Powis's fat stag dropped down dead in front of the hounds. Surely it is time that these exhibitions were put an end to, time honoured though they may be. How much better that the heroes of the day should be the United Pack, and that a good fox from Powis Castle Park should be the theme of his lordship's after-dinner oratory, rather than a fat carted stag.

FOURTH WEEK, November 16th to 21st.

A broken week, in which Jack Frost has held sway for three days, an usual occurence in November. On Monday the Shropshire were at Coton Hall, between Whitchurch and Wem. A cold frosty morning, that gave out hardly a particle of scent, consequently the Coton foxes, in their usual tactics of crossing the London and North-Western towards Prees Heath and back again, had a most successful exploration, which will benefit their understanding on the next occasion that hounds put their powers to the test. Some youth astonished the master and field by letting fly at a rabbit, when much bigger game was in the line of fire. Luckily his aim was not sufficiently deadly for any harmful purpose, but he really was not a safe person to be entrusted with a gun license. Twemlows then afforded several foxes, but these also divined that the absence of scent was an excuse for staying at home, and so after making a pretence of going Hawkstone way, and afterwards venturing towards Sandford, this unsatisfactory day was brought to a conclusion.

Tuesday, Wednesday, and Thursday were blank as I have said from frost. On Friday the Shropshire were at Wem Station, in a damp, cold, thawing atmosphere, with the plough land " carrying." A good fox in Broughton Gorse, and who that knows Shropshire does not recollect the hairy fences and wide ditches abounding in its surroundings, opened the proceedings. Luckily for the majority, hounds never ran really fast towards Baschurch, leaving Middle on their left, and were fain to give him up at Petton, Mr. Lonsdale not persevering, because Sir Watkin was due here to-morrow. A pretty hunting run, declared those on good jumpers. Thatcher got a nasty roll, owing to his horse trying to run through one of these yawners, and his horse fell on him I fear. At all events, as the sequel shows, he was unequal to getting into his saddle on the morrow. Loppington in the afternoon did not produce a fox—it seldom does. On Saturday, by common consent, all the world and his wife went to Baschurch. In fact, Baschurch Saturdays appear as if they were going to take the place of our old Whitchurch Saturdays. If I began to give a fashionable list of the patrons of sport to day, I should be taking a leaf out of old " H. H.'s" articles in the field, who bolsters up a blank day with the Hertfordshire, or a calf hunt of the Baron's, with half a column of well-known hunting names. Suffice it to say that from the Marquis of Cholmondeley downwards it was a large gathering, in which was numbered a large Shropshire contingent, that deserted their own pack at Shawbury. Sir Watkin was still absent, much to the regret of all. He has returned to Wynnstay from Brighton, and is better, but the doctors still recommend rest from over exertion, and in this bitter east wind sort of weather he does wisely to leave the reins of mastership in the hands of his brother.—

ALFRED THATCHER.

Well, I am not getting to work. Stanwardine Gorse was the order of the day, and thither the large cavalcade went. Foxes, of course, were on the move in this favourite convert, but for twenty minutes the pent-up energies of the field had to endure a cub-hunt, which did nothing to relieve their feelings. At last away he went, and crash went the charge of cavalry in the rear of the pack. Unaccustomed, however, to the din of such a multitude, it took scarcely ten minutes for this little fox to get back home again, and not all Lockey's endeavours could make him leave it again. Another half-hour was cut to waste, and then a move was made to another of the pretty little coverts that Mr. Sparling so assiduously preserves for the honour of Shropshire. This time it really looked like business, for hounds dashed away, with a wicked will, for four fields—indeed, watches made it seven minutes—and then they seemed to falter, and scent died away instantly. This sort of intermittent fun was destined to put its black mark on the day, and although one of the many foxes that was disturbed fell a victim, the real doings may be written down as nil. No! not quite, for Mr. Sparling's table and sideboard groaned with luncheon, to which he implored (not altogether in vain) his friends to partake of. An evening draw at Wettermere, Ellesmere way, proved unavailing.

Meanwhile the despised Shawbury was the scene of better fun. Here a very diminutive field, by comparison, met Mr. Lonsdale, and faces grew longer still when Thatcher did not turn up. His fall on the previous day having turned out more serious than expected, so Booker, the first whip, had to take the horn, and away we trotted to Poynton Springs. A good fox is generally at home here, and to-day was no exception. A quick eye viewed him across a ride, and he was off like a shot on the Shawbury side, and then bearing to the left, did not touch Shawbury Heath, but kept on parallel with the main road over a stiff line, and at a good pace, till we found ourselves close to Sunderton Farmhouse. Here, for the first time, hounds put down their noses on the plough, and Booker lifted them to a holloa near the keeper's house, which the hounds declared to be a delusion. Thus ended a pretty little

gallop of about seventeen minutes, on which there was
plenty of room, and to spare, for those who cared to go.
Shawbury Heath held one that jumped up in view, and
hounds were in the same field with him to start with.
No time to take a dive into Sir Vincent's gorse, so leaving
it on his right we went a rattler to Hardwicke, to the
right of the house, and into the road as if Grinshill was
his point, but the invariable turnip gatherer was here,
and he swung back into the plantations only to be forced
away again over the road to the left, and across the
railway—a nice little boundary fence with a fair ditch
on the landing side, gave the hounds room, and stopped
the ardour of a new pink—over the big fields towards
Preston Gubbalds we flew merrily until our fox suddenly
changed his mind when within two fields of it, and
re-crossed the railway near the factory, to the inevitable
Hadnal village, which appears to have a charm for these
Shawbury foxes—hounds hunted patiently through small
enclosures and cottage gardens, but eventually came to a
stand, and we failed to mark him in anywhere, although,
no doubt, he was not far off, as he never crossed the
turnpike road. All, except a few, now went home,
while the lingering hope of another gallop on what
appeared to be a good scenting day, took the remnant,
Borderer included, to Matthew's Coppice, in the east
corner of which there were a brace that took some
persuasion before one of them could be forced to leave
his comfortable quarters. When he did slip away
towards Moreton Corbet we had a pretty start; but, alas!
the scent of the morning had gone, and in a few fields
the fun of the day was over, and not a bad one either.
Booker, probably, had never hunted hounds before, so
that it was trying him high on this occasion. I trust
Thatcher will soon be all right again.

The presentation to Lady Boughey of her own and
her husband's picture on Wednesday, at Wolverhampton,
by the Earl of Bradford, was, I hear, in every way a
success; but, speaking only for myself, I should have
preferred to have seen it given at a lawn meeting at
Aqualate or Weston Park. Never has there been a
more deservedly popular gift.

There has been another marriage in Shropshire! Mr.

Robert Swan, as well-known in Yorkshire as in Sir Watkin's hunt, has taken to himself a wife, Miss Wright, of Halston. By way of doing the thing in true sporting style, and with a dash of old Halston days, the newly-married couple arranged to do Darby and Joan from the wedding on horseback to Adcote, where they were to spend the honeymoon. I wonder whether their horses' manes and tails were tied up with white ribbons for the occasion, to make the thing quite correct! Would not pillion have been better?

For the next nine days not even the huntsman's horn will tempt many a sportsman out of the arena of politics. What an excitement reigns in Shropshire and Cheshire! The squires are just beginning to realise that "the cat is among the pigeons."

FIFTH WEEK, NOVEMBER 23RD TO 28TH.

What can a truthful chronicler say of the week that has just passed, except that it has rained and blown pitilessly almost every day?

Perhaps it was the turmoil and passion, the clashing and dashing, of the opposing electorate armies that upset the barometer, or perhaps these storms were sent us by our American cousins to cool our ardour, or increase the difficulties of the situation.

Anyhow, one side have thus far come out of the fray more jubilant than the other.

Is it because they are accustomed to take wind and weather as it comes, provided only that hounds run fast and straight?

My readers must not expect, therefore, to hear of sport in the hunting field—for one fortnight such as this they have plenty of other excitement to fill their minds—but after this week, how we shall buckle to, and ride politics into oblivion.

On Wednesday Sir Watkin was at Bettisfield—not an enjoyable place at any time, but when it leads you instanter into the Fens, and those Fens are immoderately soaked, imagine, dear absent ones, the blackness of peaty mire that had to be waded through, especially when foxes declined to leave their pigstye, even on account of Wynnstay persuasions. Blacko in the afternoon, gave forth a degree of mirth to the proceedings, from which a fox ziggzagged towards the Fens, and then to Iscoyd—perambulating here for some time, then towards Bubney Farm, and then ringing again, the staying division eventually found themselves at Blako once more, after various adventures by flood and field, and crossings and re-crossings of the canal and railway, which made the day one of the most crooked of the season. Although keen men declared it was an hour-and-a-quarter to ground on the railway at Alkington.

This aforesaid Wednesday saw the Shropshire at Dorrington Station, alas! still without Thatcher's horn. The proceedings may be summed up very shortly as far as sport goes. Plenty of foxes in Acton Burnell coverts —fog too thick to see which way hounds went—no use trying to get down into the lowlands—wet, weary and disgusted, the field soon left Booker all to himself. I wish I could end the story of a poor day here, but, as a matter of fact, how often we find disaster in company with disappointment. A lady, whom every lover of foxhunting in Shropshire admires and honours, braved the elements on the off chance of a run, but not on one of her accustomed horses. The brute suddenly bethought him that his coach was at home, and that he was on the spree Putting thought into action away he went, and before he could be steadied a biggish ditch intervened. Here, swerving first, and then pitching on to his head, his unfortunate rider fell on the right side. Her riding habit hung on the pommel of the saddle, and she was cruelly dragged for some eighty yards, the beast that had caused the mischief kicking at her in the meantime. Could anything have been more dreadful? Indeed, we have known so many similar accidents turn out fatally, that it is comforting to know that, with a presence of mind truly wonderful, the prostrate form put up both her arms to protect her head and thus saved her life, as her arm was severely kicked and only one cogmark of a shoe was planted on her head. We all rejoice that she is recovering, and will not be permanently the worse. Moral: Every horse to his trade, especially where a lady is concerned. When shall we have a really patent safety ladies' pommel?

Friday, after a terrible night's rain, brought a certain amount of sunshine and a softer air, but with scarce a calmer atmosphere. The Shropshire were at Hardwicke Grange, where Mr. Bibby has diligently tended a lot of foxes for the season's amusement, and not allowed them to be slaughtered during the cub hunting. In the absence of the Master, Mr. A. P. LLoyd did the double duty of Master and huntsman, Thatcher being only present on wheels. Hardwicke Gorse did the needful without any delay, and the fox, after much heading, made good its exit across the railway to Hardwicke Park, then back again with more chorus of men than of hounds, leaving Hadnal village on his left, as if for the Gubbalds. Running parallel with the railway, however, nearly to Battlefield, they once more re-crossed it, and eventually found themselves at Haughmond Abbey. Not a bad point—and certain choice spirits were fain to sing praises of the gallop, which the man in a balloon tells Borderer was somewhat of a delusion—holloa to holloa—and very little hunting about it. Anyhow, the same tactics were pursued back by the Ring Bank, and eventually nearly to Hadnal village, where no further intelligence could be gleaned. Had hounds really run to-day with the ground in its present state, what a scatteration of ardent sportsmen there would have been! In the evening from the Forge coppice, close to Moreton Corbet, hounds ran really prettily up to Sir Vincent's gorse, where Booker lost trace of him.

On Saturday, at Aldersey, I understand Sir Watkin had a pretty good day, of which, I trust, you will hear particulars shortly. That beautiful Cheshire vale must for once in its life have ridden heavily—and the Aldersey brook was a foaming chasm, I should say!

For the last three years the Severn has not rolled down such a flood as it now does. Let us hope it comes on purpose to wash down all the mud that the elections have heaped on its fair surroundings, and that, as it slowly retires within its banks, into its wonted quiet meandering, it will point a moral to our upheaving passions, and aid us to fall back into our wonted paths of usefulness and every-day life. Borderer can stir the fire, but he likes it extinguished better.

SIXTH AND SEVENTH WEEKS,

November 30th to December 12th.

I was faithless last week owing to unavoidable circumstances, dear Eddowes, and whether your readers will be indulgent enough to forgive the loss of their usual weekly dose remains to be seen. A naughty boy is willing to promise anything that may cause him to escape punishment, and I will call to my aid the old Eton rule by pleading "First fault."

December the 1st, oddly enough, shone brilliantly on the two old-fashioned hunts of the county—the Wheatland and United Pack. Mr. Summers, with the former, is winning his way gallantly. He found his pack and country at sixes and sevens. Difficulties had to be encountered that had shipwrecked more than one aspirant, but he has thus far shown himself equal to emergencies, and a decided sportsman. I can assure him that there is no reason why he should not bring back the palmy days that I recollect of old, when Mr. Baker, before he went into Warwickshire, made the Wheatland country famous in the West Midlands. On this memorable Tuesday the meet was at Faintree Hall. A fox was found in a gorse at Neenton, that if he really was the hero of all that followed, must have been an extraordinary example of stoutness. He first of all made Chetton his point, and then bearing away to the south, chose a fine wild line, with very little plough in it, and plenty of dingles and obstacles in it until he reached Stottesden, and then skirting Kinlet, eventually beat his enemies in the interminable fastnesses of Bewdley Forest. A glance at the map will show that this run could scarcely have been less than a twelve-mile point, and at times the pace was good.

This part of the country carries such a holding scent. Two-and-a-half hours was its recognised time.

The United on the same day met at Newcastle, about three miles west of Clun. Their first fox did not stand up long before them, but their second was a real denizen of Clun Forest. Found in Cwmbryth Dingle, he at first made for Mainstone, then coming round on the high ground by the Three Gates, crossed the Whitcot bottom, and kept on his way steadily eastward till he came to Bicton and the Berry Ditches, a tremendous stronghold, of no avail to him to-day, however, for the deathlike music at his brush drove him on to Walcot, and, too hot to enter Lord Powis's woods, he struggled on towards that famous hosterly, the Purslow Hundred House, and died in one of the coursing meadows there, at the end of an hour-and-a-half or thereabouts. Anyone who, like myself, knows the country, can appreciate what a fine hill run this was, and how wonderfully it must have brought into play the perfection of horse, hound, and fox. How the green coats and black caps must have whoo hooped over him!

There is only one bright spot in the Shropshire week that I would fain recall to memory, for its record must not be lost. Middle is a favourite meet, and Friday, the 4th, saw Thatcher again in the saddle, with plenty of eager sportsmen in his wake. The Park wood is generally a pretty sure find, but to-day it failed. Merrington, however, at its extreme point on the Leaton side, held a fox that luckily was prevented going there, and made sharp tracks for Middle, affording plenty of fun for a few short minutes ere he got the better of the hounds. A couple or so of hounds were reported to be running towards Pimhill, and his line became the next attraction. It proved but a stale one, however, and soon had to be given up. Then came the cream of the day. Preston Gubbalds at once announced itself a holding covert, and the fox, cut off from his usual road crossing into the larger part of the wood, had to take the open Albrighton way, and then pop into the covert lower down. This bit of experience so sharpened him up, that, contrary to the usual tactics of these foxes, he went straight through towards Hadnal, and while many a knowing-one was lingering on the right, hounds were fairly flying parallel with the London and North-Western Railway for Hardwicke Gorse and the Black Birches. "Thank God," said the persevering ones, "for a hard high road," which helped materially to catch the hounds, and put all into a good humour, as they flew on by Nevitt's plantation, leaving Yorton Station on their right, and soon brought the horsemen with extended pipes to Broughton Gorse. Here it is averred that foxes were changed. The one that went away with the pack at his brush looked fresh. There having been no time for getting second wind, Sleap Gorse was passed, and the Ellesmere road nearly touched, when he bethought him of hospitable Petton, and, cutting round to the left, ran the boundary of Sir Watkin's and the Shropshire country with extraordinary cleverness, giving the rear division a chance to cut in and have the inside of the circle. Every fence and ditch here are sneezers. The black soil luckily rode loose, and not so holding as in drier weather, but still those really with the hounds were few, and the dirty coats many. Petton proved an impossible haven for him to-day, so he tried for Middle Park, and a few fields further, at the Harmer Hill Quarry, he was cracked up in good style, after fifty-five minutes of brilliant going. This gallop, I think, takes the first place in the Shropshire season so far, although Borderer hopes it is only an augury of still better things to come.

I have picked up no news of especial interest about Sir Watkin. His last Baschurch Monday before the frost put its hard mark on the country, was, I hear, pleasant, but of no extraordinary virtue. One fox was killed in the Adcot shrubberies, and another Nesscliff way. Plenty of dashing about, but no real straight going. Lockey, I hope, has recovered from his nasty blow in the mouth which knocked out his teeth, a serious thing to a huntsman, who has to be continually blowing his horn. While I write the frost is disappearing beautifully, the week's meets read temptingly, and I may be able to put in a postscript of yet one other day before this diary closes.

P.S.—My promised postscript shall be forthcoming. A nicer hunting morning than opened on Monday, December 13th, never gladdened huntsman's eye. The frost had taken its departure like a lamb, and the air seemed to breathe a scent. West Felton, with Sir Watkin, could not be resisted, especially when a friend offered a charming mount. Sandford Pool was our first draw. I have seen a larger gathering at this well-known covert, and several habitual faces were absent. How they will curse their luck when they hear of our doings! Across the road at the head of the pool came our fox, and all had a fair chance of starting down towards Prado, hounds at once told us that there was a scent, then swinging to the left, he hesitated in Lord Bradford's covert, and was nearly caught. Away again over the road, leaving Sandford Pool this time on his left, we went like pigeons towards Knockin; then inclining right-handed by Shelvock, we raced over the grass, skirted the Old Baschurch Steeplechase Course, just touched the lower corner of Grigg Hill, and had a beautiful line in front of us with Nesscliff his only chance of safety. Not destined, however, to be reached to-day, for as we pass the brick-kiln hounds catch a view—for one other field it is a course, and he is caught close to Ruyton—a more stylish finish I never saw. Thirty-five minutes and a most enjoyable gallop. Grigg Hill soon put life into the day again—a fox going away quickly towards Knockin, and then wheeling on the high ground took us by Shelvock Farm, and straight down the flat for Boreatton, but his life was not destined to be a long one, for ere he reached the brook at the far end of the course, hounds ran into him. I believe a sheep dog had had a hand in the business. He was a big fine fox, and should by appearances have gone on beyond those short fifteen minutes that we had chased him since leaving the hill.

Once more our luck was in the ascendant, for no sooner were hounds in LLoyd's gorse at Shottaton (where was the owner to-day?) than a good fox was away grandly with his head straight for Nesscliff. Surely this time we were in for a turn here. No—for after giving us a stiff trial of hairy fences, when close to it, he swung to the left and went for Ruyton Church, over the very spot where perhaps his relation this morning had yielded his brush. Here in spite of annoying hollaas hounds worked on beautifully, and Eli Skinner, in the absence of Lockey, showed himself to be a huntsman, as in obedience to the master's wish he let them alone. Grigg Hill delayed hounds, its gorse is so thick, and a little time was lost in getting away to Shelvock, where he was viewed, and we pegged on after him over the brook towards Prado, then right-handed in front of Tedsmore House, in the plantations beyond which we got up to him. Once more there was a rally, as he made a last dash for his life down towards Rednal, where he, too, yielded his brush in a cottage garden. The third dog fox of the day, and all caught in the open. No. 3 had kept us going just an hour. It was only two-thirty p.m., but all voted it *quantum suff.*, and turned happily and contented homewards. Well done, Mr. Walford—plenty of the animal in your coverts—and to-days victim will soon be replaced, let us hope, by some new comers, of even better wind than their predecessors.

EIGHTH WEEK, December 14th to 19th.

The hope of bringing the Grand National Hunt Steeplechases to Shrewsbury in the spring has been dashed to the ground, the committee choosing Malton by a narrow majority. Unfortunately two or three of our friends could not attend, and hence the adverse vote. Yorkshire has already had these steeplechases at Wetherby, while Shropshire has never been similarly honoured. Your readers will, however, be glad to hear that the directors of the racecourse are by no means disheartened, and that they intend the cater for a thoroughly enjoyable meeting in April, when each and all the local hunts will have chances distinguishing themselves, and a carefully-prepared programme will very soon be issued, which will embrace steeplechasing and flat racing in equal proportions, and an effort is being made to time it with the Ludlow Club meeting, so that a regular old fashioned Shropshire week will be the order of the day when hunting is over, and the country houses will be full.

The little fox terriers at the show last week were a

pretty lot. Plenty in number, but small, it struck me. I suppose it is the fashion. I saw one with a cock-up ear and marked for a prize : surely this was a mistake. Very few looked capable of tackling a fox, much less a badger. The two prize hunt dogs from the Wheatland and Ludlow interested me most, but then I am not a judge of fancy dogs.

Hunting has been in full swing, and the elements have been fairly propitious. A bubble long in blowing has burst at last ! Harmlessly too, I believe, although it was popularly supposed to be charged with dynamite. All true friends of sport breathe freer I believe now that this Hodnet fulmen has been allowed to puff off. The correspondence has been published, and no one, I am sure, believes that Mr. Heywood-Lonsdale took the hounds as a political engine, or that by taking them he has influenced the politics of North Shropshire. No fox hunter, whatever his politics, will, I am sure, deny Mr. Lonsdale the free right to his political opinions, so long as they do not interfere with fox-hunting, and I can truly say that never have politics been introduced into the hunting field by Mr. Lonsdale. In the present case, I think the master does all that a rich man could do to facilitate sport, and not give offence to any. He asks for no subscription in North Shropshire—he has purchased kennels—he has done the thing in a princely way—and yet (I say it with shame and grief) he is the subject of treatment which would severely try the temper of some hot-headed M.F.H.'s that I know. Surely, however, there is yet sufficiently good feeling left among us, impelling us to throw aside politics, and stand by our Master so long as he nobly and honourably stands by us.

And now to the more genial topic of sport.
Tuesday the South Cheshire had perhaps the most amusing and eccentric day of their season, as with a good scent they galloped madly between Wrenbury and Cholmondeley in the semi darkness of a fog, much oftener hunting Mr. Corbet than attempting to ride after his hounds. Much tumbling and fun resulted, which to the more sober fox hunters must have been a delusion, and the afternoon in Combermere proved no better than the morning.

Wednesday took the Shropshire to Loton Park, their extreme westerly meet now that the Wollop is given up. The fun will not take long in describing, although with luck a first-rate day might have resulted. Loton Withy Bed held a brace of good wild foxes. One broke on the upper side, and took a splendid line up the meadows towards Ford, when hounds suddenly threw up, and could make nothing of it. Back to the withy bed went Thatcher to get on the line of another, or perhaps the same fox that had returned. Away they went again, really only a portion of them, for five couple had cut off the fox and driven him over the river Severn unseen, except by a few, and they had to look on, while alone in their glory, these five couple flew away to America! No bridge for five miles, so there was nothing for it but to send a whip after them, and go elsewhere to draw again. This was vainly done, the district never being particularly foxey. These five couple had a clipper to Nesscliffe, and the whip nearly spent the night there trying to stop them, so numerous were the foxes in front of them.

Thursday at Gresford I hear Sir Watkin had a good day, finishing near Holt.

Friday, the 18th, Mr. Heywood-Lonsdale was at High Ercall. A good meet that always draws. The Duke of Cleveland's large farms here give plenty of room for everybody, and when the ground is damp holds a good scent. To-day the Ouse covert did not hold, but a little wood near Ercall Park was more fortunate. The fox at once dashed down to and through the river Roden, much to the consternation of the field. The only handy bridge is a brute of a thing, narrow, weak, and positively dangerous. To-day it caused a block and nearly collapsed. The lucky ones first over sat down to ride through as quick a thing as has been their lot this year, having to take in their stride some big and wide places that intervene between there and Poynton Springs, to get to which they made a bit of an elbow towards the Ring Bank. Straight through the Springs, the field tailing tremendously, past Shawbury White Gates, then to the right, leaving the village on the left as if for Moreton Corbet; but without reaching there, they soon found themselves at the Lea, at the end of about forty minutes—a most enjoyable spin, which virtually ended here, as Thatcher failed to hit him off, towards Preston Springs. Those with second horses went on to Wytheford, and Morgan's Pool, and saw them drawn blank—then Ellerdine produced a bad fox that did not add to the evening's enjoyment. Can nothing be done to improve that horrible bridge?

Saturday, the 19th, all the sporting world of North Shropshire and South Cheshire went to Hinton, where Mr. Peele Ethelstone always provides a welcome and foxes without end. Whitchurch, too, turns out to see the fun, and it would take a keener east wind than blew to-day to have kept the eager throng at home.

Of course hounds were soon at work, and ran down towards Quoisly, then back to the eternal Peele's Gorse, which as usual kept the field in shivers and impatience for fully an hour, when for the twentieth time the hounds had to be called off, and a stay-at-home Reynard triumphed. I long to know what the secret of foxes' dodges is in this little Erebus. Ossmere produced a brace, one of which was caught in covert, and the other went away to Combermere as usual, and was run out on the Marbury side and lost. Ash Gorse is generally the *bonne-bouche* of the day. It was two-thirty p.m ere it was reached to-day. Not a whimper disturbed its recesses for another ten minutes, and then away he goes to the bottom. The throng at the gate is let loose, and those wide rushy pastures are once again the scene of a superb gallop. Taking the centre of the vale, eastward—it is not for Cloverley that he flies to-day, nor for Combermere—fence succeeds fence, and hounds still fly over those lovely three miles ere Shavington great red wall confronts you. The wags declare he is a Tory fox, for he shies at the wall instead of seeking the sanctuary within it. Sharp to the left, parallel with it, bang comes a brook to be jumped or tumbled into—a few preferred the latter process, or rather their horses refused to do their best. Burley Dam is left on the left. Kent's Rough is whisked through cleverly, Adderley is entered, and the house and park passed through ere this capital fox manages to save his brush in one of Squire Corbet's hospitable earths. The Squire is there himself to join in the fun, and is brought home in the style he loves best, smiling to think that his fox is safe, and probably it will be his turn next to rattle him back over this superb line into Sir Watkin's country. The run was thirty-five minutes, or perhaps a bit more, and crowned the day with another feather in the cap of my dear old friend Ash Gorse, and its *fidus Achates*—Mr. Frank Cotton.

NINTH WEEK, December 21st to 26th.

The past week has been a full one. A green Christmas has been vouchsafed to us, and the boys, home for the holidays, have had a rare time of it.

Monday, the 21st, at Prees Station, was one of those bright balmy days that this capricious climate of ours sometimes brings us in mid winter; when a great coat is an incumbrance, and the air breathes light and joyous. A conglomeration of Sir Watkin's and Cheshire men came to swell the happy throng that were soon put sharply on the move from Lacon Gorse, on the Coton side of the railway. Getting very well away with their fox the hounds raced straight past Prees village. The line is a stiff one, and the railway throws you out of gear. Few, consequently, enjoyed this quick thing to perfection before the fox was pulled down, in fifteen minutes, near the village.

Twemlows was the inevitable second draw, and a fox was viewed away over the heath, hounds moving prettily to Ightfield, where they checked, and Thatcher held them back to the Twemlows. Here, after some more drawing, a fox or foxes kept them going in a very round-about in and out sort of fashion, for two hours, till all were tired except the foxes, who lived to fight—let us hope a straighter fight—another day. Opinions differed about the day—some said, pretty good, others the reverse.

On Tuesday, the 22nd, I understood Mr. Corbet had a good day from Adderley, notwithstanding the fog. A good fox took them nearly to Market Drayton, then to Styche, and finally got to ground near Little Drayton.

Wednesday, the 23rd, the Shropshire were at Dorrington Station, on the South of the Severn. A pretty good field turned up in spite of the unfashionableness of the country. In this, however, Borderer does not agree. People must be very fastidious who cannot enjoy themselves where coverts are small, grass predominates, and the lie of the land is a gentle slope towards the Longmynd, five miles away. To-day we began badly. In the absence of the master, and there being no one in *loco magistri*, Thatcher had written orders to go after some depredating fox at the Thresholds, at least five miles of stony road from the meet. When we got there, a few dozen fir trees surrounding a small pool was all that could be seen of the fox covert, and it appeared very unlikely that even for one chance day in the year would a fox make it his home. Ill-tempered, therefore, we jogged back four of those rugged miles, and at twelve-thirty began to draw in earnest for a fox towards Netley, for I should tell you that Mr. Llewellyn, the owner of the intervening covers at Stapleton, sent to stop our drawing them. He is great at setters, but sets his face against hounds. Well, there was soon an end of our grumbles when we came to the Shady Moor. The bitch pack settled on a good fox at once, and rattled him due westward up to Underhill. We found ourselves out on the Cothercot Hill, pointing for the clouds, but our fox was not quite such an excelsior as this, for, turning to the right, we dipped into the inclosures again and found some of them boggy enough, as two men at least could vouchsafe, and surmounted the ridge which revealed to us the Gatton valley, with Lord Tankerville's mines and the Stiperstones in the foreground. A large covert—Huglith—on the hill side held us some quarter of an hour, when there was a tallyho at the top of Westcot Hill, and whether it was a fresh fox or our hunted one, this deponent cannot say. In either case the result was a very fast spin back into the low country, from which we had emerged in the morning, the line taken being a better one, and the comet-like proportions of the field spread over its expanse most interestingly. In about forty minutes we were back at Netley, with our fox turning and twisting ominously, when a false halloa most perversely came, and saved his life, after a run of an hour and forty minutes from the find. An evening fox from the Corfield coppice took them across the railway to Gonsal and Condover Park, there darkness, with sixteen miles home to kennels, made a departure imperative.

Thursday, the 24th, brought allurements for hunting men at Walford, and New Street Lane. The Shropshire drew largely at the former place from a section of the Wynnstay people, while Sir Watkin himself, on his extreme Market Drayton side meet, drew the South Cheshire and North Stafford men into his field. The Shropshire had but a poor day. The Walford spinnies failed. Merrington was supposed to be blank, although a fox slipped away unheeded. Fitz Coppice came to the rescue, but the field were on the wrong side and headed him from his best point. As it was he slipped back, and gave a ring of a few fields out by the church, and then went to ground. An unpolite fox in the afternoon disturbed the Leaton lunch party, by choosing that inopportune moment for poking up his nose in the home drive. His journey, however, did not extend much beyond the home circuit before he had made himself scarce.

Sir Watkin found a leash of foxes in Styche Gorse, the hounds declining to forsake their close attentions to one, while another good looking one went away. However, No. 2 had to go or die pretty quickly, which he did towards Shavington, then vainly endeavouring to get home again was met by the rear guard and driven across the road, hounds settling down ran fast towards Styche Wood, but not entering it kept on to Cloverley Pool, through the park and out by the lodge gates, over the big pastures as if for Sandford. Here, however, we seemed to cross another line of less flavour, for, after a few fields in the neighbourhood of Bletchley, we got slower, and soon had to give him up, although our hunted fox was scarcely out of view leaving Cloverley. A trot back to Cloverley Wood did not produce a fox, and then they went to Shavington, where they found, and brought a fox away to Styche and Cloverley, but the afternoon got very dark and foggy, and none were very sorry when Sir Watkin had the hounds stopped about three-thirty p m., and home became the word. I thought it a good scenting day, and the first bit in the morning was pretty, hounds hunting merrily.

Friday being Christmas Day, we all ate and toasted each other, talked hunting, settled the affairs of the nation for another twelve months, and prayed for a fine month of January.

Saturday, the 26th, brought us the inevitable Boxing Day meet at Battlefield—a soft balmy day—as mild as May. It is needless to say, therefore, that thither went a goodly proportion of the townspeople of Shrewsbury. It was gladdening to see such a gathering in these supposed degenerate days when sport is said to be doomed. To Borderer's mind it gave the contradiction flatly to such absurdities. Give the British people a chance of a holiday, and I will undertake to say that with all the allurements of pleasure within their grasp, the majority will choose the hunting field, even under all the drawbacks of Shanks' pony, greengrocers' carts, or shandridan four-wheelers, if horses cannot be found, and will enter into the sport *con amore*. To-day the rank and fashion of town and country were well represented, and if ever a day was made on purpose, as well as the foxes, for affording fun to the holiday makers, Christmas 1885 was the day; curiously contrasting with that of 1884, when the hounds never came on account of the frost, Thatcher aptly remarking that he had hardly slept for the past twelve months from remorse at that disappointment. A fox was going directly, that tried to cross the line, and was of course, headed. He proved, however, a cripple, and in five minutes was made an end of. He very soon had a successor, who got such a chorus as certainly never fox had before at his brush, in his face, on all sides of him. Neverthless he dashed over the railway and road, and made good his retreat towards Sundorne, although we unaccountably failed to hunt him when he took the open. Back to Battlefield, where another brace were soon going, and playing the same game of crossing and recrossing the railway, being headed in the road beyond, until one went away to Battlefield Church, and pushed himself past a grated drain, which said grate swung on hinges it turned out. Clever little fox that, to be able to push open the door and let it close after him. Now it was time to leave the foot people, and try Preston Gubbald. Coffee housing had been the order of the day, but a find in Preston Gubbald somehow or other generally means business. It is such a good scenting covert. Away he went on the Hardwicke side, while another broke on the other side (I saw six foxes during the day), skirted the Black Birches, and up the high ground at Nevett's plantation. Here, sharply to the left, he brought his long line of blowing pursuers to Pimhill, barely touching the side of it, he took us by the Gubbalds Church, and ran a complete ring outside the scene of our departure. He would have gone to Hardwicke, I think, but the road was full of carriage people, and he had to come back to the wood, where the chorus became deadlier every instant until, to save his brush, he pushed himself into a rabbit hole, from which he was dragged out and killed.

How often I wish I had an inventive turn of mind! To those that have, here is a grand chance, not only of a fortune, but of the united gratitude of the hunting-lady world. Think of that alone, and do something to make the pommels of a lady's saddle or her riding habit be separable quantities, when desired! Thrice this week have accidents happened to ladies from getting hung up in their saddles in our hunting circle. Fate has, indeed, been too cruel to one, who has often tempted it successfully, but who twice last week had to part company with her skirt, as her only safety valve—luckily in her case it was so—or her accident would have been terrible. More terrible than the enacted tableaux of a shorn lamb, which some kind friends, and a veiled prophet of Korassan were said to have witnessed! In the third case, on Saturday, the catastrophe might have been still more serious, but for the behaviour of a favourite horse, who refused to be frightened, while its rider hung over on the right side, firmly dangling from the pommel, and the habit refused to give way, or unloose its frightened burden. It took several pairs of strong arms and hands to set matters right, and we all join in exclaiming " All's well that ends well," and thus ending this year, 1885.

TENTH WEEK, December 28th to January 2nd.

I could not be ubiquitous last week, and am indebted to a friend for the following excellent account of Sir Watkin's Boxing Day meet, at Iscoyd, and the North Staffordshire sport at Woore on the following Monday :—

On Saturday, the twenty-sixth, there was of course a large gathering of holiday folk at Iscoyd Park, the seat of that cheery old sportsman, Mr. P. W. Godsal. Every available nag in and around Whitchurch had either been hired or borrowed, and I heard of one sportsman who actually had to hire a gee from Tarporley. Well, our first draw was the snug cover at the bottom of the Park, but as many foot-people had assembled round the cover before the hounds were thrown in, and a brace of foxes being awoke from their slumbers a little earlier than necessary, took the hint that something more than usual was going on, and made the best of their way towards safer quarters. Our next draw was the big wood at Kiln Green, and a fox was soon on foot and away over the Parkley Farm, past Whitehall Chapel, leaving Oak Bank to the left, and over the road below, pointing as if for the Fenns, but, turning to the right, he ran as if for the middle of the Wyches, but again turning to the right, leaving Tybroughton Hall to the left, we ran past the Higher Lands, over the Kiln Green Farm (near to where we found), then on past Wolvesacre Mill, and to ground in a small dingle at Agden. A man with a ferret said he would try to bolt the fox, but the tables were turned, the fox made the ferret bolt; in fact, from what I could see Mr. Ferret's bolt was shot. Digging was then tried, but an eight-feet stick failing to reach the end of the earth, the fox was left in peace. This was a slow hunting run of about forty minutes. During the run some of the hounds marked a fox to ground in a drain, while the body of the pack went on with our hunted fox, so from Agden we went to this drain. A terrier at hand soon bolted number one, who ran right into the jaws of the hounds. A further perusal of the drain discovered number two. He was soon dislodged, and made the best of his way, with one hound in very close attendance, into Kiln Green Wood, just two fields away.

Here he dwelt for some time, and eventually broke, but only to run into the nearest farm stackyard. He was seen to go into the stackyard, but not a soul ever saw him go out, so the question arose, "Where can he be?" Well, an old hand (we heard him described as a vile old fox-slayer) was seen riding quietly about amongst stacks and turnip "hods" and at last he detected a hole at the bottom of a door out of the stack-yard into a portion of the buildings. He said, "The fox has gone through that hole, judging from the clean appearance of the floor" and true enough Reynard was there. Rustic number one, on being asked to search failed to find him, but rustic number two said, "If he is in here I'll find him," but the fox found him first judging from the way rustic number two gave tongue. Having dispatched this "rat of a fox,"—for he was found in a drain and killed in the farm buildings, we proceeded to Scholar's Wood, close to the Wyches. Hounds had drawn the cover when a whimper was heard, and in a very short time the whole pack opened. The cover being small the fox was soon away, and so were the hounds, and they ran at a good pace up to Agden, skirting the dingle, where we had run to ground in the morning. From Adgen the line was to Grindley Brook, then over the canal and railway past Mr. Ethelston's of Hinton, over the Tarporley Road, and up the hill, as if for Peel's Gorse, but suddenly turning to the left, we ran across Mr. Nunnerley's farm, and down into the valley, as if pointing for Barmere, but poor Reynard, being hard pressed, turned to the right, no doubt to seek the friendly earth on the Quoisley Farm, but although within a stone's throw he failed, and was pulled down after a capital burst of thirty minutes, and that over a country that foxes seldom take from the Wyches side.

North Stafford, at Woore, on Monday the 28th. The night had been very windy, although free from rain, consequently the chances were that foxes were stopped "in" instead of "out." Can Ridding, Ten Brooks, and Arrows Wood all proved tenantless but not so a "Court of Chancery" Wood Mill Hayes by name. Well, all I can say is this, that if the Court of Chancery would only get as quick through its work as this fox was in quitting their property, a great relief would be felt to many. Good fox! He did not wait for any affidavit to be filed to say

that he was about to quit, but quitted on his own accord, ex red tapeism, running with a very fair scent. We ran round Peewit Hall, then back, close by Admiral's Gorse, then straight for Dodington Park, but just before getting to the Park he turned to the right, and ran through Checkley Wood, out on the far side, then into the wood again, through the middle of the wood, and out on the Crewe side, and was eventually lost in a storm about two miles away from Checkley Wood, on the Crewe side. Dodington Park covers were then drawn, but proved blank. Then we had a trot to Admiral's Gorse, but although we found a fox, if not a brace, there came on such a storm of hail and rain that the hounds were ordered home.

Sir Watkin, at Whittington, on Monday, enjoyed good sport. The day, however, was rendered famous by the fox doing the cats' trick so cleverly that it took a rustic all his time to climb up the ivy tree and dislodge him. It is indeed hard to disassociate the old story of Whittington and his cat, from the proceedings of the day—not that there is anything wonderful in a fox's going up a tree—hundreds of them lie in trees by preference, especially when the country is wet, and the woods get thin or are much disturbed. An old tree fox is very hard to find, and is generally a dodger. I have known them when hard pressed go to ground in a hollow tree, and scramble up inside it. The editor of the *Morning Post* was so exercised in his mind over it that he indicted a leading article on the subject there and then. How much more remarkable, however, was the hopeless exploit last week of the East Sussex fox that went out to sea sooner than do battle with Mr. C. E. Egerton and his pack any longer. The Whittington fox must have known well the voice of Colonel R. Lloyd, of Aston, and had no doubt often winked his eye at him from above. He lives, I rejoice to say, to amuse us, and on the next occasion, when he is called upon to *come down*, may I be there to see.

On Tuesday a bitter north wind and snow storms put in a decided veto to much sport, although several packs tried their best, and old Alec with the United succeeded on Wednesday, notwithstanding the snow, in having a capital run over the hills at Church Stretton. The Shropshire did not venture from their kennels, and small blame to them, for in the morning the travelling was dreadful.

Of Thursday, no tidings had reached me, but Friday burst upon us as a day of good omen for the new year. Jogging to covert was hot work, and the sight of some lambs (Dorsets), then in a field by the roadside ere we reached High Ercall, made us think strongly of the latter days of February, and sigh to think that already the season was three parts over, with none of those glorious days to gloat over, which mark an epoch in a hunting man's existence.

A very large field were attracted by the morning, the place of meeting, and the idea of distinguishing themselves on New Year's Day. Happy greetings rung out so aptly, that it might well be said of High Ercall that it was in high feather, and full of go on this spring-like opening of A.D. 1886. The long cavalcade moved off to Rowton Gorse, certainly the snuggest abode of foxdom in Mr. Lonsdale's country, well chosen apparently in every way for showing sport, as there is not another covert near it, and a bold fox cannot take a bad line from it. And yet how often has it been a base deceiver to the fond hopes of many of us? I can count up several days when I have gone down to that brookside full of hope, only to leave it in disgust. To begin with, the gorse is so thick that foxes decline leaving it, and when they do they seem to have only one idea, and that is to get back there again. My experience of Rowton Gorse foxes is that they are the worst in England. There were a brace there to-day which never put even their noses out of the place, and, after twenty minutes' ferretting, managed to get to ground, thus crushing our morning's hopes. I may be fastidious about giving a fox a chance at starting and placing the field at the covert side, but I am free to confess that were I empowered to arrange the drawing of Rowton Gorse, no horseman should go into that lower field adjoining the gorse, at all. The buzz of two hundred horsemen close to the gorse, and on the very side where the black thorn cover joins the gorse, and is the natural place of exit and entrance of the fox in his

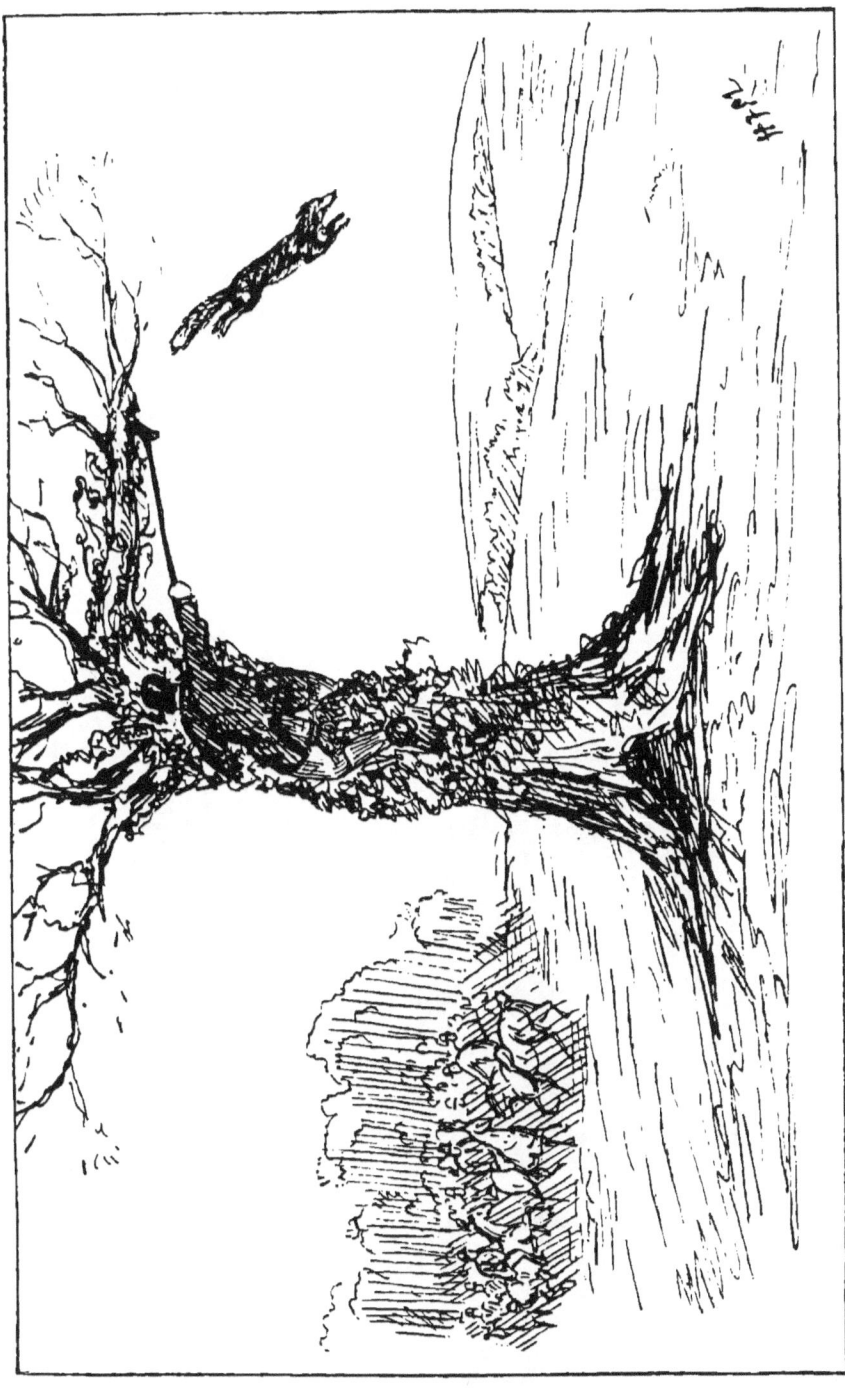

nightly rambles, bothers and disconcerts him immensely. Everyone would get quite as fair and quick a start if they remained on the hill above, or, better still, if they were taken past the gorse to the railway side of the covert. The Shropshire field are getting notorious for their straggling, and to-day they certainly surpassed themselves. Before Forester's Plantation was half drawn a great part of them were in full sail for the Marle. Bad luck stuck to us throughout. There was a flash in the pan at the Ouse, and a fox at home in Wytheford, which went away well across the Roden to the Forge Coppice, after which but an uncertain idea of his whereabouts could be gleaned. Borderer thought he went Hawkstone way, as he was unlikely to face the wind blowing in his face Acton Reynald way. Perhaps no day of fairer promise gave forth more delusive results than our New Year's Day, 1886.

Sadder, too, when we heard of an excellent day on this self-same Friday over those delightful Carden pastures, the particulars of which I failed to cull—and the same must unfortunately be said, to a lesser extent, of the Wheatland at Wenlock. My correspondent there must be presented with a new set of very sharp spurs, as a reminder that his pen is not that of a ready writer. A quick find, I believe, in the lower end of the Edge Wood took them nearly to Easthope, then away towards Weston and Brockton, where he turned to the left for Bourton, and eventually beat them close to Spoonhill. The first part was very fast, and the whole made up a good hunting run. Overton, however, is not good at accounting for his foxes. How many an old Wheatland man wishes to see Alec back again !

The Albrighton have been doing more than their share in the way of sport, which I grieve to have to pick up second hand.

All accounts agree in making Saturday from the Plough, Weston Heath, a first-rate day—while the elements spoilt their Penkridge Tuesday, and Newport footpeople mobbed a good looking Loynton fox; still "Croppie Boy" maintains that the old Albrighton never went better, and Borderer only wishes that he could be at Coppenhall on Tuesday to judge for himself.

The Radnorshire, too, had a good run on New Year's Day from Norton Manor, and its owner, Sir R. Green Price, Bart., was there enjoying the fun on his cob, riding after his eighty-third year, as the old story goes.

I have to turn my back on Baschurch (Petton), but this shall only be a pleasure deferred, as far as my readers are concerned, for an eagle-eyed friend will hover over that wide expanse of rough pastures and black ditches, discerning everything to its minutest details.

ELEVENTH WEEK, January 4th to the 9th.

How much we are governed by local circumstances, and hence how hard it is to bring oneself to write of hunting when all around wears a mantle of snow, and King Frost reigns supreme ! Still I am in duty bound to try. We left off with the first day of the New Year. The next day brought better luck to the Shropshire than they had experienced on Friday. Starting close to where they left off, or ought to have left off, had Thatcher followed his fox to his legitimate point the previous evening, Besford Hill, was the first place of attack. Here there was a fox that gave forth so little scent as to be of no use in the way of sport. The Rubbishes produced one of a still worse sort that was soon slain. Acton Reynald Park, however, put a brighter complexion on the prospects of the day. Here a good fox was in waiting, and went away over the wall and across the road into the Rubbishes, through it and on over the open, almost passing by the tempting haven of Preston Springs. Entering it, however, on the Wem side, he made but a short stay before quitting it at the same point, and taking a capital line towards Wem. Just, however, before reaching Shooter's Hill, he shot to the left nearly to Yorton Station, then more to the left up the hill past Clive, and at the back of the Grinshill quarries to the Rubbishes, which were destined to shelter him no more, and it was an expiring effort that took him into Acton Reynald Park to die close to the happy hunting grounds of Sir Vincent Corbet. It was a fast

SIR VINCENT CORBET, BART.

ring of one hour and eight minutes, over a very fair line, that could not fail to please its votaries. I regret very much to hear that Sir Vincent himself got a nasty fall, which laid him on the shelf for three or four days. People don't fall lighter as they get older, and it is gratifying to know that he is none the worse. Still more gratifying, in a foxhunter's point of view, is it to have such a practical refutation of the stories which have been banded about, that our leading squires were going to give up fox-hunting and preserving foxes. There was not, I believe, a member of the Corbet family who was not enjoying the sport on Saturday in one form or another, and no one can say but that Sir Vincent's coverts have been full of foxes all the season. Of those that went best to-day, Mr. Walter Corbet, Sir Richard Sutton, and Mr. Clement Hill certainly deserved the credit of having cut out the work. Sir Richard, it is clear, inherits the bold blood that was famous with the Quorn some twenty odd years ago, and which will always be identified with Skeffington Hall, as much as with Lord Lyon and the Derby.

On Monday, all the world and his wife went to Baschurch; that is, the world inhabiting the Great Western line of country from Wrexham to Shrewsbury—the Whitchurch and London and North-Western side choosing Coton with the Shropshire. Petton being the order of the day, Mr. Sparling soon showed them foxes in plenty. Stanwardine Gorse behaved better than when last visited, a good fox going away beautifully. For the first ten minutes the crowd had to race, and very soon there was no jostling. Hounds ran past Cockshut, as if for Loppington, and then, turning right-handed, ran to ground at Burlton Mill. After the first ten minutes the pace became slower. Petton again produced a plethora of foxes, one, if not more, of which were killed without much fun of a decided character. Those happy men with second horses, I understand, had a run in the evening, of which I hope to glean more anon. I hear that B. and S. had the best of the first run—not Brandy and Soda, my dear friends.

The Shropshire and Coton, midway between Wem and Whitchurch, had much fun to boast of. A stay-at-home fox in Coton Gorse had to pay the penalty of his cowardice, and, no other fox being at home, a trot was made to the Twemlows. On Lord Hill's side away went a fox over Prees Heath, in the middle of which he turned to the right as if for Whitchurch, and at such a rattling pace did the pack chevy him over this open ground, with no fences to stop them, that, although he tried hard to reach the earths at Ash, in Sir Watkin's country, where he would have been safe, he had to succumb within two-hundred yards of them in nine minutes! The Twemlows had been too much disturbed to afford other foxes on the return there, so Losford Coppice was the hope of the afternoon, and who that knows this snug cover, and has enjoyed many a good gallop from it, does not light up with earnest hope as hounds challenge in it. It is to be a dash at the brook at starting this afternoon? or is the line over those fine, wild pastures, with unkempt, blackthorn fences, that intervene between it and Hawkstone? Ah, yes! this question is soon decided. He turns his back on the brook, and sails away gaily for the sure haven of the Grotto. Now gentlemen sportsmen! whose hearts among you are bent on business? Now is your time; not a moment for hesitation; there is a flaming, screaming scent, and the Shropshire bitches are second to none in England for pace. Ah, who says that Thatcher can't ride to his hounds? Look now how he hesitates not a moment; and how those two bits of black—they are Hills—hang on his quarters, and know every inch of his hairy vale, struggling with might and main to be in the same field with him and the hounds. Why here is the Hawkstone Road, in less time than it takes me to write it—in eleven minutes—and where are the field? Still those bitches fly on to the Grotto, to ground —twenty-one minutes in all. What a superb gallop!

On Tuesday, Mr. Corbet, I hear, was not able to do a great deal against the negative elements, although from Wenbury Mosses his followers had a short excursion or two, as long as scent, which was very fickle, lasted. Several coverts Marbury way were drawn blank, and a bad fox from the wood by the Mere soon ran into a stable yard, and was killed. Poole's Gorse was the last chance, and a fox from there going towards Combermere could hardly be hunted at all, so full was the air of cold storms. Certainly, Mr. Corbet has been most unlucky with his weather on Tuesdays.

Wednesday in most places was a white world that precluded all idea of hunting. I can answer for its being impossible in Worcestershire, as Borderer's intentions were centred on the Croome and had to bear a disappointment. Nevertheless the Valley of the Severn, west of Shrewsbury, was favoured, and there was nothing, I understand, to stop hunting at Loton. Having put my foot into it by giving a wrong description of events at the last meet at Loton, I will keep clear of details now. Suffice it to say that, if my information is good for anything, no vestige of a fox turned up till Preston Rough was reached, and a fox here popped at once to ground. Bickley Wood held a brace, one of which went away very prettily for the Holyhead Road, over it, and on towards Onslow, without touching it, however, or Preston Rough, he was hunted to Ford, where he went to ground, making a slow hunting run of twenty-five minutes, albeit the line he took was a good one, and with that earth properly stopped next time this fox may afford us a clipper.

News from the Ludlow side has not been abundant this year, a stray leaf or two has reached me lately, which leads to the belief that sport has mended considerably. There was a good sporting day from Tugford, while from Kyre a successful incursion was made into North Hereford country to Marston Firs and on to ground near Docklow. About a fortnight ago a new little covert in the vale near Staunton Lacy was the scene of an exciting gallop over a nice line, past Culmington Manor, round the Monument and back again, down to the Corve near Delbury, eventually killing him opposite the abode of that good sportsman Mr. Wood, at Culmington Manor. Milson Wood has also afforded a run to Newnham and Gaudywood; and old Norton's Camp held a good fox last week that took them to the Edge Wood and Hazeldine. I hear that some more United blood is being infused into the pack.

And here my chronicle necessarily ends, as the elements have put down their foot decidedly against us for some days, I fear, and it will be cruel indeed if the Hunt Ball, as well as its rival at Berwick, should be disappointed of hunting attractions at Berwick and Atcham as a sort of second course in the festive week.

Of hunting accidents still the crop seems to thicken. Mr. Drake, in Cheshire, had a severe shaking a few days ago; and the Duchess of Westminster has been added to the list of fashionable ladies who have been hung up by their saddles, stirrups and riding habits having an unhappy knack of refusing to part company, when their rider's lives depended upon it. I am happy to hear that, in the Duchess's case, her horse behaved like a Trojan, and she was not dragged or kicked. Borderer is almost tempted to re-produce, with slight variation, the remarks of a certain "Gentleman in Black" on ladies' habits, written twenty-four years ago. If the frost continues he will certainly do so.

TWELFTH WEEK, January 11th to the 16th.

The entries for the Spring Handicaps remind us that we are past the meridian of our hunting season, and soon shall be face to face with the March winds. As soon as the weights are out we may have a prophetic peep at races such as the Grand National Steeplechase. Our Shrewsbury Spring Meeting is not yet published, but Borderer has permission to say that, in addition to races under Newmarket rules, there will be an open hunters' steeplechase of at least £100 value. The Shropshire Hunt Cup of 50 sovs., for farmers and tradesmen in the Shropshire county, given by Mr. Lonsdale. A United Hunt Cup of 70 sovs., open to residents in Shropshire, Staffordshire, Cheshire, Worcestershire, or Wales. Two hunters' flat races, an open hunters' steeplechase, of 70 sovs., and another selling hunters' steeplechase; so that there ought to be no lack of sport in the way of hunters' races on the 8th and 9th of April, and we hope to see

AN UNACCUSTOMED FEAT.

plenty of competition for the Shropshire Hunt Cup.
Every horse must be owned on the 1st of February in
the country to qualify him, so there is not much time to
look out for likely ones. My weekly jottings of sport
begin with Wednesday, the 13th, at Berwick Hall, when
the frost had most accommodatingly cleared away, and
left the fields once again safe enough for the indulgence
of the lovers of Terpsichore to shake off the effects of
Tuesday night's, and Wednesday's early morning's
dissipation at Squire Watson's, where, I understand, even
a fuller and gayer assembly than ever enjoyed themselves
on the opening day of the new Parliament.

Wednesday broke a very wild morning, quite enough
to drive foxes underground. A tremendous assembly of
nasty, fresh kicking horses after the frost, filed off to
Hencote Pool, where, nicely sheltered as it is, a fox
had braved the elements above ground. He put his
nose for Albrighton, or rather Battlefield way, and the
first three ploughed fields fairly planted the majority of
the field. Not crossing the Wem road, he went up to
Albrighton Hall, and wheeled back again, luckily more
on the grass now, but at an indifferent pace, to the
place of departure, or hard by it, where all trace of him
seemed to vanish. Perhaps he went to ground. Here
ends all chronicle of sport for to-day. No fox at
Preston Gubbalds, Pimhill, or Harmer Hill. Plenty
about, but underground, Borderer imagines.

On Thursday Sir Watkin repeated his good fortune of
Wednesday, when in the afternoon of his Overton Bridge
day, he had, I believe, a very interesting hunting run
from Campbell Gorse, over a lot of country, eventually
running to ground in the Wyches. Well! on this
Broughton Thursday, although some of Mr. Howard's
coverts had been disturbed the day before, a fox was
seen travelling from Grafton Gorse, that took them
over a line of deep meadows, rotten after the frost, that
made jumping in and out of them a matter of immense
difficulty. There was a brook, too, by the way, which
was too much for Lady Cholmondeley's made hunter,
luckily without hurt to its charming rider. Without
touching Castletown, back they went to Broughton,
where he managed to dodge them and get to ground.

Largess was the evening find, and again a deep line was the chosen one to Cherry Hill and Chorlton, then on to the eternal Wyches, by which time those who had not already had enough of tumbling, scrambling, and cramming, pounded after Lockey, until he eventually, like a good determined huntsman, killed his fox, I believe, in the shades of evening. A good hard day.

On Thursday night, according to custom, the young Hunt Club of Shropshire gave its annual ball. Borderer was not a sharer in the entertainment, and he fears now, like a burnt child, to take even ball news second hand. A desperately long list of grandees filled the columns of the next day's paper as present, and judging by the number also that turned up at Atcham Bridge on Friday morning, I do not think our county balls have in any way deteriorated from their pristine grandeur. How devoutly one wishes to be young again, just for a season or two, to see whether the young people do really enjoy themselves as much as of yore! Well, as I have said, to Atcham Bridge came a very gay crowd—north, south, east, and west were represented. Ladies by the score, so much so that a stranger whispered, "Do you always have so many ladies as this out?" Sir Thomas and Lady Boughey were there, I am sorry to say, on wheels, and the master of the Albrighton had little opportunity of looking over my favourite bitches before a move was made to a covert outside Attingham Park on the Wroxeter side. This held nothing, so on we went to Ravenshaw Gorse, and here again we were disappointed. Our cavalcade seemed by this time to have no end, as we filed away back for the park, just as it began to rain steadily, the usual Atcham downpour. The Park Wood was drawn blank, and much to the disgust of many members of the hunt away we went at the Wroxeter gate, straight back along the road over the bridge, on and on past Cronkhill and Berrington, to Eaton Mascott, when hopeful eyes had been turned towards Longnor, or Holly Coppice. Borderer does not pretend to know the rights, or the ins and outs of these matters, but the arguments of the north men seemed cogent when they exclaimed that Holly Coppice had not been drawn since cub hunting. Anyhow, a master has a

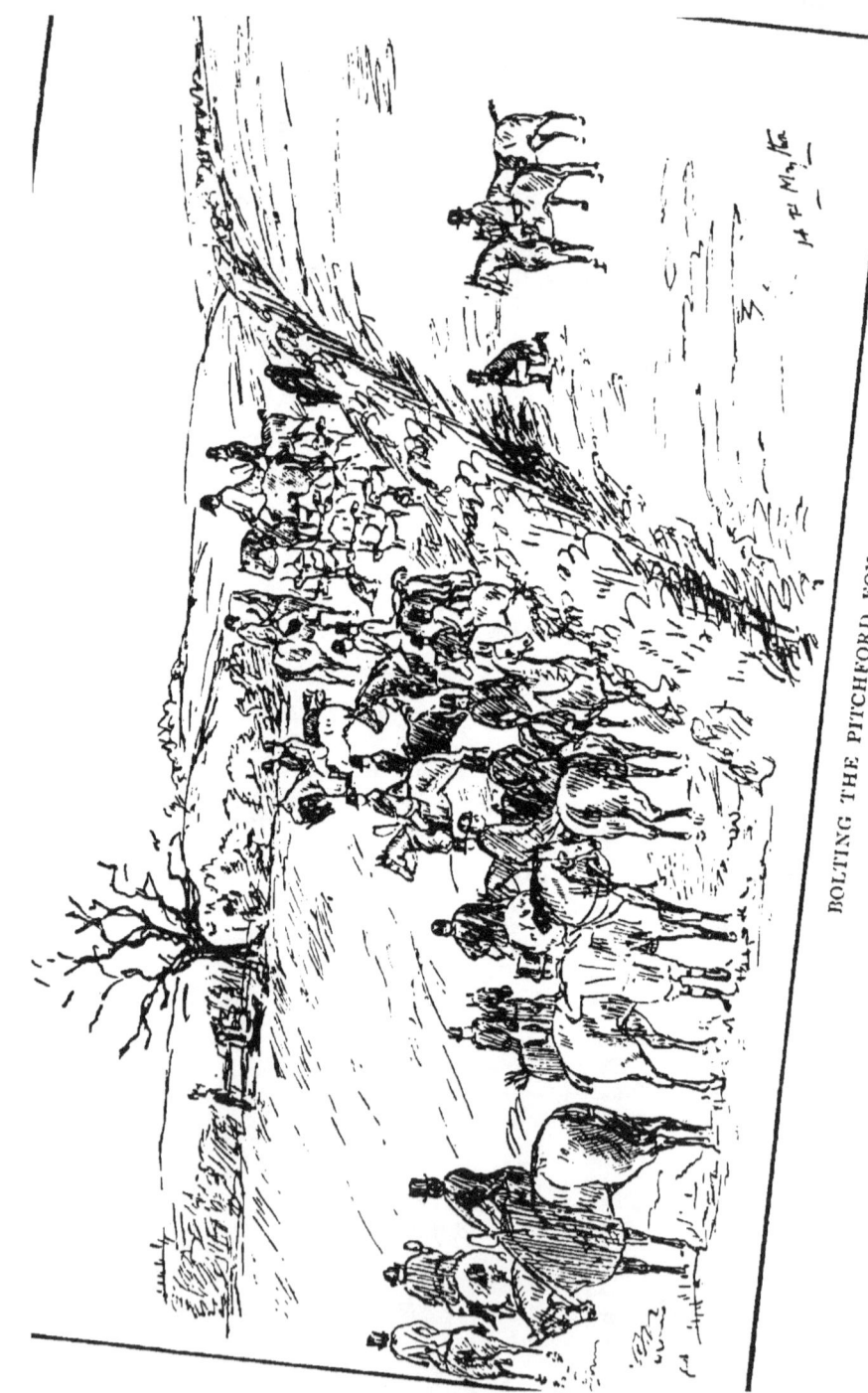

BOLTING THE PITCHFORD FOX.

right to make his own draw, and so on went the
majority with him, and soon saw a fox found in the
dingle there that had the hounds tied to his brush down
to Cound Mill, and just as we thought he was going
over the railway to give us a sharp chase, he disappeared
into a big pipe drain. A young sportsman keen, but
not alway discretionary, doubted the fact, whereupon
Thatcher. not given to betting, offered to stake his
year's wages on it. This caused his opponent's betting
book to return to his pocket instanter. There was
nothing for it but to trot to Golding Coppice, and there
we had as pretty a find as possible. Luckily the field
were not so much spread about, or as unruly as usual,
and the fox got, I thought, well away right handed at
the bottom of the covert. A boggy brook at the end
of the second field caused fun, and some grief, while
hounds ran like wildfire to Eaton Mascott Dingle, and
then turned up to the left. Whether some extra speedy
ones managed to out-gallop both fox and hounds, and
head the former, I don't know, but before he reached
the head of it he was made mincemeat of—a second
unlucky bit of business. Two scrambling "no-goes,"
of ten minutes each. Nothing daunted, on we went
to Pitchford Hall. The day had improved. It was 3-30
p.m., and Colonel Cotes quietly suggested that his
terrier should be invited to try a drain within a field of
the hall. So in he went. I had had scarcely time to
admire a Chippendale yearling when—" By Jove, he is
at home," and out he pops, as nice and healthy a fox as
ever was seen. He scarcely has a hundred yards start
as the hounds race him in view into the big wood.
With what a crash they send him to the top end. In
trying to get away he is headed by some men at work in
the field, and back we go over the dingle, and down the
other side. Ah, now we are really away at the bottom
corner to the right, and pointing for the Lawley for a
few fields. Now swinging to the left, we skirt Sir
Frederick Smythe's model farm, and his clean cut fences
are nice jumps—over his private drive, and still bending
left-handed nearly to Steven's Hill, where we cross the
Cressage Road, for Harnage Grange, and point for the
higher ground, Bull Hill, I think it is called. How

sweetly the bitches hunt him; plenty of music, and all doing their best. Straight on to the top of the hill, not far from Kenley, where we check in the road, or rather the junction of roads. It is a ticklish moment. Has he run the road? No, for'ard over the plough beyond, and before half the field are aware of it hounds are racing for Hughley, with the Edge Wood, a long dark line, in the foreground. Many a longing eye is cast back towards Shrewsbury now, as the list of defaulters is numerous—the soil is holding and the fences blind. "Come up you beast. Thank heaven for that leg to spare." Now they turn straight up the dale, and our fox sees that here at all events there is no rest for his failing strength, so once more he turns his face for home, and goes back by the Lodge at Church Preen, and right up wind to Netherwood. It almost looks like a fresh fox, and yet that deadly crash of the not to be denied bitches speaks a different tale—out at the bottom for Frodesley Hill. It is too dark to see them, but lovely to hear them. "Get on, sir," says a farmer, "they're close at him." The hill is too much for him, he turns by the side of the dark fir plantation with the wall round it, once more crosses the road, and there is only that big ferny field between him and Acton Burnell big wood. Can he reach it? The bitches are within fifty yards of him, he has to turn, and there under the low wall by the Rookery Farm, they bowl him over, just as the clock is at five p.m. So dark is it that it is hard to see who is there, and who not. One hour and twenty-two minutes by the master's watch, and a first rate finish to an unpromising day. Barely a score of the mighty two hundred that congregated at the meet are there to witness the end; to their honour, however, be it said, two ladies of our bluest blood, coming from the Ludlow country are there to claim the trophy of the brush. They put all our home belles to shame; one has to catch a train for Bromfield. How we all wish her brother was as fond of hunting as is this young lady. It is a long time since Pitchford has shown a better run than this, and it was really good form in Colonel Cotes putting us on the track of this good fox, as

he did. I hope he is none the worse for getting planted at that deep uncovered drain, Hughley way. I hear the Wheatland gave up at 2-30 p.m. to-day —early for a young master!—and that the North Stafford did not essay to hunt at all.

THIRTEENTH WEEK, JANUARY 18TH TO THE 23RD.

The majority of people think that frozen-out fox hunters are discontented mortals. This is true of a few only of them, especially those who have a dozen or so horses in their stables eating their oats in idleness, and whose resources do not lie in the direction of business, or other sports; whose arrears of work that have been put by for a rainy day are happily not to be found, and to whom *ennui* and frost are synonymous. These Borderer pities, and for them he cannot prescribe a remedy.

I promised, when the frost came, to cut a leaf out of the old "Gentleman in Black," for the benefit of my readers, especially the ladies. He wrote just a quarter of a century ago, and was *facile princeps* in his own special line. With a particular strain of blue blood in his veins he moved in the highest sphere of his day in Leicestershire, and for piquant, pointed writing on any subject that he had made his own, he equalled if not excelled, Whyte Melville.

I do not make myself responsible, ladies, for his opinions on "Ladies' Habits." Here they are.

"I fear, now that I have written it, that the title looks a little alarming. To attack what women, and what habits is the natural question that suggests itself, as 'The gentleman in Black' puts lance in rest. Be assured, ye more lovely daughters of lovely mothers it is your riding habits only. Or may I not speak more correctly, and call them habits of riding, transferring my censures from your costumes to your customs. Feeling, as every man of gallantry must, an interest in your welfare far beyond expression; knowing, too, how that welfare must be bound up in the creation of certain feelings in our sex, forgive me, if I venture, at this stupid season of the year, when those wretched debates have scarcely commenced, when everything cheerful is in Leicestershire, when the spring is setting in with more severity than usual, if I occupy a little of my own time and your attention by entering upon an important, but delicate question. How far is woman fulfilling her mission by adopting some of the attributes of the other sex—more especially in the matter of sport ? Do not, fair ladies, imagine me ignorant of the fact that there is much to be said on both sides. I have not now to learn that wherever you are concerned there is certain to be something to say; and usually it is very well said. But listen to me first, and dispute with me afterwards; and if I am unable to retract, your opinions shall be treated at least with all the respect they deserve.

"There is so much that is charming, so much that is elegant, nay, so much that has an appearance of tenderness and delicacy in the connection of a pretty woman and her horse, that I am almost afraid of being mistaken when I combat the abuse of a companionship calculated to exhibit both in a charming point of view. But, surely, no one means to assert that Lady Nancy Bell by the side of Lord Lovel, in Rotten Row, reining in her milk-white steed to a pace which accommodates itself to the intellect or conversation of her lover, is the same person we saw coming neck and crop at a hand gallop over the rails at the bottom of Loseby, or swimming about in the brook below Cank, when she was only preserved from extremities by the assiduities of a ploughman and his team. Look at her now, every band of that beautiful hair in place; her soft white hand bared to caress her favourite Selim; her faultless form, lithe and lissom, retaining its upright carriage, only to move with her horse, as his lengthened stride proclaims his power and temper; the folds of her graceful habit undisturbed by a passing wind; and her brow unruffled, uncontrolled by a single frown; and you have a picture of womanly delicacy and ease, not more than equalled by the repose of———as she smiles her languid smile from the soft cushions of her barouche. Look at her again; her rigid figure thrown back, or leaning constrainedly forward; her hair looking as if it belonged to no particular parish, but had a claim upon all; her horse covered with mud, and herself not entirely free from a participation in the same defilements; her beautiful face flushed with something more than the rudest glow of health, not far removed from perspiration; her lips stern and compressed, and her forehead wrinkled with the determination to 'do or die;' that graceful cutting whip with golden handle, exchanged for a more manly hunting crop, wielded with considerably less elegance, and with an energy always misapplied. And here it must be admitted that I have taken the most lenient view of the case; here are no broken bones, no tumbles, no torn habits, and discomforted head-dresses to repair. The entire picture is one of every day's occurrence, and as faithful an account as the Amazonian tactics of the present generation will permit. Have we returned, then, or are we returning, to the days of Mrs. Flint and Mr. Thornton?—I beg pardon, I should have written Mrs. Thornton and Mr. Flint. Who is there amongst us who is ignorant of that dashing performance which took place in 1804 at the end of the York Meeting, when one-hundred thousand persons assembled on Knavesmire to see Mrs. Thornton ride a four mile match against Mr. Flint? Verily, they were matches in those days; but they were not women. It is, still, the only match I should have felt inclined to make with the lady. It is not enough that women be pretty, let them be women. *Et quocunque volent animum auditoris agunto.* Indeed they then may lead the mind of the hearer in any direction: then they may act the part I have attributed to them above, and curb that licentiousness of thought and freedom of manner so characteristic of a certain class of our young Englishmen. But where in the world is the happy influence of a woman in a leopard body and blue sleeves exhibiting herself amid the excitement and applause of a Yorkshire mob? Who would like to be driven instead of led by a young lady in buckskins, be she never so lovely, whose only object in married life is to hang up her husband over a hog-backed stile, and to be laming his horses, when she ought to be at home rocking the cradle? This material adaptation of male attire to feminine recreation should be reserved for *les esprits les plus forts*, and though I am unwilling to admit that the metaphorical wearing of those habiliments by the ladies saves an immensity of trouble to the male sex, true delicacy is quite incompatible with the exhibitions of them.

"I cannot but hope that these lines may occasionally meet the eye of the wives and daughters of those gentlemen, whom we boast to be our chief support, the sportsmen of England. I apologise most sincerely if I hurt the feelings of such persons. My criticism is not directed against them. To a lady equipped and mounted, in whom the *mise en scène* presents the perfection of horse, of hand, and of appearance, I can only say, as my favourite poet,

> Pictoribus atque poetis
> Quidlibet audendi semper fuit æqua potestas

I do not love this universal passion for the chase, which has extended itself amongst all classes of women. Half of them know little or nothing about real horsemanship, they are deficient in judgment and power, and have nothing to offer in exchange but a courage the offspring of excitement and ignorance. I know few things so painful to my nature as to see a badly-mounted, bitted, or habited lady in the hunting-field. It is difficult to know whether most to pity the man to whom she is attached, or herself. If she be good-looking, so much the worse—one regrets the more the incongruity. She cannot escape observation except by doing what, unfortunately, so few will do, trotting about the lanes, and returning home as soon as the business of the day begins. If ladies who were meant for pony chairs or four-wheelers will insist upon riding, let it be as modestly as possible. But this will not do; as we remarked before, Tom has his two or three hunters, and dear Bella her palfrey—*Bella horrida Bella*. Then Bella must go to see the hounds just to look at them; and Tom's friend will look after Tom's sister as there is no groom; or he has to clean the plate or wait at table in a scratch establishment. Then Bella gets enamoured of the riding, ventures into the fields, has a little jump, then another; and seeing Lady Dina, who has about six-thousand a-year, and a perfect horse, saddle, groom, and hatchet, with every necessary appurtenance for destroying property, Bella naturally thinks how easy it is to do the same.

She invests in a slang peajacket, and hammer-headed hunting whip, and a hard-looking chimney-pot. She imagines that a bridle is a bridle, a saddle a saddle, and a horse a horse; that a gentleman riding well a-head of of you is just the same as a well-dressed groom in attendance, and that a devil-may-care fling, all on one side, at a greasy-looking hole, where the odds are two to one on a fall, is the same thing as the finished performance of Lady Di. Lady Di is the single exception, Bella Smith the hundred-headed monster who startles our propriety in half-a-dozen shapes every time we put on our boots and breeches. The Bella Smiths have become so numerous of late that it behoves honest men to tell them the truth. If they can afford a good-looking hack, and have sufficient taste to dress themselves well; if they have brothers who can put on a bridle and saddle as it ought to be, who will curb the taste for colours and ribands and buckles, and who can induce their sisters to sit straight upon their horses, there can be no possible harm in their exhibiting themselves from twelve to two p.m., between the 1st of May and the end of July in Rotten Row. They will have plenty of admirers and a legitimate basis for admiration. Or, if they prefer it, there can be no harm, under the same irreproachable circumstances, in riding to cover every day from the 1st of November to the middle of March, providing only that plenty of sea-room be given to those whose business it is to look after the hounds and not after the women. But there is one conclusive argument which should exclude the sex, as a rule, from the dangers of the chase. On the score of humanity alone, we deprecate any display of equestrian power beyond that of the simplest kind. To see a woman crossing a country with that resolution for which some of them are famous gives me a cold shudder compared to which total immersion in Wissendine is a warm bath. I know the insecurity of the whole thing from beginning to end; the uncertainty of everything sublunary, excepting a woman's seat, which is so dangerously secure that, in case of a fall, she can scarcely get away at all. The best of horses, the best of men, occasionally come to grief. Does that pretty woman bear a charmed life only because she does

not know where to have a fence, and because she allows
her horse to go with reckless indifference at all alike?
Is she never to fall, only because, if she does not make a
mistake, she has no power to recover herself? How
lately we have seen the reverse, and not with an indifferent
horsewoman, but with one of the best in Leicestershire.
There is a trusting confidence about a woman in most
things, which is one of her greatest charms, but when
extended to an unwarrantable length with horseflesh it
becomes a dangerous attribute. Perhaps she makes an
unflattering comparison between us and her four-footed
favourite; she may be right. But let me suggest that,
if her confidence in man has been misplaced, it should
make her something wary of such unlimited trust in
anything. The pitcher goes often to the well but comes
back broken at last. And what a terrible smash it is
when it does come! If you handsome women only knew
the number of hearts that are beating for you every time
you indulge in what you call pleasure bear compassion
for our feelings would curb your aspirations, and confine
you like unruly graduates, to gates. If ladies will hunt,
let them have a pack of hounds and a country of their
own. A *lionne* is a terrible animal; the first step to
adopting her nature is the pursuit of the fox. If Miss
Kegelspiel chooses to ride like a centaur, and talk like a
cabman, let her; it's nothing to anyone. Do you, young
ladies, pity the sorrows of a suffering sportsman, who is
wellnigh driven from the field by your temerity. Do I
speak strongly on the subject? Pardon me. I have a
family of daughters who would all like just to see the
hounds meet. I only hope they take in *Baily's Magazine.*"

Forgive me, ladies, if my "Gentleman in Black" has
hit too hard! We know that in Shropshire the Lady
Dianas far outnumber the Bella Smiths, and that the
quarter of a century since he wrote has done much to
tame the savage minds of the male sex in the hunting
field; and that, while admitting the soft impeachment
that may come home to us now and again, that ladies
occasionally are a dread and a terror to us in the hunting
field, how often, on the other hand, are we not constrained
to admire and welcome them, even when not riding in the
lanes, and how much they tend to humanise us in this,

the almost only national sport in which they can partake with us on nearly equal terms. In spite of the "Gentleman in Black," why may not the true fox-hunting lady (I wish there were more of them who could honestly and sincerely lay claim to the title) say equally with her gentlemen friends, in the words of dear old Bromley Davenport,

> Oh, glory of youth ! consolation of age !
> Sublimest of ecstasies under the sun !
> Though the veteran may linger too long on the stage,
> Yet *she'll* drink a last toast to a foxhunting run.

FOURTEENTH WEEK, JANUARY 25TH TO THE 30TH.

The only means that I can devise for getting back into the good graces of the ladies, after quoting last week the criticisms of "The Gentleman in black" on "Ladies habits," is to go a step further, and give the gentlemen a turn of the same screw. This will show an impartiality on Borderer's part, which must commend itself to all fair dealing persons, irrespective of sex, age or prejudice. The following little episode I quote from as great an authority as the gentleman in black—it was written exactly at the same time, twenty-five years ago, by an eminent sportsman :—"And now we come to the field—a large heterogenous body of horsemen congregated at some fashionable meet, rather with the object of killing time than of seeing a fox killed—sporting men—not sportsmen—who know no more of the noble science than they do of the Japanese language, and don't care a straw about the working of the hounds. All they care about or want is a gallop. The fact is that the great majority of the present generation lack the earnestness of their sires in all the business of life, save money-making or spending it.

"They go out foxhunting, because it is the fashion, but are neither earnest in their love of the chase, or the love of women, reminding one of the lines:—

> What say our modern gentlemen :
> Do Cupid's darts with poison fills us?
> Oh ! no ! They tickle now and then ;
> But hang me ! if they ever kill us.

'Well, Tom,' asked an old sportsman of his son the other day, 'what did you do from Tinker's Hill?'

'Quick thing, Sir, for twenty minutes—pace quite awful—lots of fellows came to grief. Fences, Sir, like green baize doors—couldn't see through them. I shan't show again till the leaves are down.'

'Yes, Tom, the hedges are very green for the time of year; and so I suppose were more than half your field as to their notions of riding to hounds. But what of the pack; did they look well?'

'Charming, Sir. Sleek as moles.'

'How did they work their fox?'

'Never saw a hound, Sir, after they left the gorse; except one confounded old brute, who got in my way at a bullfinch; and I believe my horse broke his back.'

'Poor old Chaunter, perhaps?'

'Not unlikely, Sir; for he opened his pipes pretty loud when I went over him.'

'Ah! that's a bad day's work for you, my boy. The squire will never forgive you, if he knows you killed old Chaunter.'

'He got in the way, Sir—just in my line, and I could not pull up. Highflyer would have it.'

'Turn aside, Tom: never ride in upon the hounds; keep always wide of the pack, as I used to do. But there, it can't be helped now. I must walk another couple of puppies for him. I suppose you made your bow to the Master?'

'Yes, Sir; confound him! And he made his to me in a way I did not quite like.'

'How so?'

'Why, I was hallooing the fox, thinking to do him a service thereby, when he rode up to me, and, lifting his hat said—Thank you, Sir, for your kind intentions, but I pay three men for doing that which you are attempting.'

'A polite reproof, Tom, for meddling in his servants' business. I dare say you were hallooing the wrong fox, and doing mischief, for which some Masters would have thanked you in different language. Well, did you see Alice Ashton?'

'Yes, at a distance, surrounded by half-a-dozen Crimean heroes.'

'Ah! she's a charming girl, Tom, reminding me of your poor mother when she was about her age; it makes my heart glow to look at her. Why, aren't you half in love with her already?'

'No, governor. Fellows don't fall over head and ears in love with a handsome woman now a-days, as they did in your time. It don't pay, that sort of a thing—marrying a pretty girl for her beauty only. Money, Sir, money is all we think of; and if Alice had lots of the needful, I might perhaps take the trouble of making advances in that direction. But as for love in a cottage, it's exploded, Sir, like that puff of my weed. *Tenues evanescit in auras*, as we were taught at Eton; clean gone Sir—out of sight, and out of date.'

'Ah!' muttered the govenor, 'things have come to a pretty pass in the old country. No wonder they are shipping cargoes of young women to the colonies. The chief object of the present generation is to kill time and annihilate space. Every man is in a violent hurry about his own business, be that what it may. Half London is under-tunnelled to save a few moments—perhaps half an hour at the outside—to meet this universal mania; the speed of the railroad is not sufficient. Telegrams are barely sufficient to pander to this morbid appetite; and in the name of common sense, to what purpose is all this inordinate haste? As if time did not flit sufficiently fast already. The man of trade tells us, time is money; that is, he considers every minute lost in travelling or receiving the earliest information on his particular matters is so much loss of money to him. Reuter's office is besieged to learn the earliest information of what they are doing in foreign parts, to serve the purpose of money-making speculation in the rise and fall of the funds; and this restless spirit, impatient of check or delay, prevades the hunting field also. 'Pace, pace, pace,' is the one universal cry amongst modern fox hunters. They say—

> Our fathers talk of hunting, let them,
> We only want quick bursts, and get them"

We have saved our blank this week, but only on Thursday was the weather passably good enough to enjoy sport.

On Wednesday the Shropshire essayed to hunt at

Lythwood. Below the hill at Bomere snow and frost had disappeared, but on the higher ground snow lay sufficient to make riding unpleasant, and, as a climax, a cold drenching rain came down unmercifully. Such good judges as foxes invariably are in their choice of dry and sheltered homes, on a day such as this, were, of course, impossible to get at, and so no one was astonished or indeed sorry, when Thatcher threw up the sponge, at two p m., without finding one.

Thursday mended matters considerably, and Whitchurch Racecourse was the rendezous of the most select field of the season, owing to the greater amount of snow that lay on the Wrexham, Ellesmere, and Oswestry side of the county. Sandford Pool covert and withybed were too wet to hold their accustomed fox, so a trot had to be made to Cloverley, which seemed full of foxes. A peregrination of a not very interesting character took place from the big wood to Shavington, and after toiling in its miry clay for a short time, back went their fox to Cloverley, and was lost. Scent did not appear brilliant, and the going was so heavy that many had the shine taken out of them before Lockey went in search of fresh foxes in Cloverley Gorse. There they were in plenty. One making a bolt for Ightfield sorely tried the humour of the field, who wanted to pursue him, while the hounds declined to leave another that took the opposite direction, and soon landed them again in Shavington. This time, however, with better intent, for he went straight on, and out as if for Adderley, but more to the left to Burley Dam and Kent's Rough, and then with a vastly improved scent, he essayed to give his pursuers a taste of his quality, and test their powers of going at high pressure through deep pasture, by steering straight for Ash Gorse. Without, however, entering it, he struggled on to his home at Cloverley, and died there, after giving them a fine ring of something over an hour, which, considering the awful state of the country, was more than most of the horses could do with comfort to themselves.

On Friday Borderer had made up his mind to carry out a long-cherished scheme of a day with the Wheatland. The meet was at Weston, right down the dale, and the nine mile jog from Bridgnorth would have been enjoyable but for a steadily increasing snowstorm, which dogged his onward track until, by the time Monkhopton was reached, it became quite deep. Wisdom, in her mood of caution, whispered "Turn back;" while desperate hope against hope said "Go on the meet at all events." So to the meet B. went, only to find there four footmen; so the friend who had picked him up on the road suggested an adjournment to Oxenbold Farmhouse, just to shake off the snow before turning homewards. Corvedale is noted for its hospitality, and here, unexpectedly, was found in the owner another friend. Mince pies and grog soon thawed us, and just as we were thinking that the storm seemed to be breaking, there came a cry of "The hounds, the hounds," and sure enough there they were, in full cry in the wood at the back of the house. To horse we scrambled, dashing through the snow, almost a foot deep, like maniacs. Never did hounds make such music in such a wilderness of snow. We plunge after them through deep, muddy rides hidden by the snow, regardless of consequences. Now they are away at the top—how can we follow? Thank our lucky star they turn back. No fox can travel in such deep soft snow as this. He only just reaches the covert before them, and again the grand chorus rings and re-echoes in every corner, as we stand and listen. At last it ceases. They have caught him—almost. He has crept under an old stubb, and hidden himself for a few minutes only to be dragged out after five minutes of determined scratching. Here is an opportunity of looking over the hounds—having a chat with the master and one or two old friends. We are only fifteen in all, and three of them ladies—simple mad men and women to hunt on such a day. "Bless you, we were out on Tuesday, had a good run, killed one fox, and ran the other to ground on foot," said the master. On the principle, I suppose, of *carpe diem* this is all right, but running after foxhounds is a game I never aspired to. "Old Mr. Turnbull had it all to himself on his cob," replied some one. I was pleased with the hounds. There yet remains a decided bit of tan about them, the pride of the country, by which old Baker used to swear. Their tongue is deep and musical, and they showed a dash of determination this morning that few foxes could have withstood. It was decided to try the lower ground. Snow here would, perhaps, lie lighter. By the time we got to Widowsfield, down it came thicker than ever, and had it not been for a chat with Wadlow over a bit of steeplechasing, and looking over his training ground, we should have been well-nigh frozen. "Come on," said my companion, "they have drawn this wood blank, and are going to Spoonhill." Where could be a better guide? So on we went to Spoonhill. No hounds here at all events. I met another of our small field, whose information led me to suppose that they were gone towards Monkhopton, but here there was no sign of them, and so Borderer, with his head to the manger, battled on through the snow as fast as he could to Bridgnorth. Three hours afterwards, when curled up comfortably in an arm chair, having regained his normal temperature, comes a knock at the door. "We all thought you were lost in the snow. Had a capital run of an hour, and stopped the hounds at Hughley; got on a disturbed fox at Widowsfield; did not go into Spoonhill; on by Butron, to the Edge Wood like mad; awful riding; huntsman got a bad fall; come dine with me." It sounded like a dream, almost impossible that hounds could have slipped away from Widowsfield without Wadlow or myself seeing or hearing them. Napping again, old B. Well, it is a sign of the creeping infirmities that we are all heirs to, that I should have been left behind from probably the easiest covert in the dale from which to see or hear. I made no excuse but went to dine in sullen silence. Under the mahogany, however, all came right again. I regret to hear that Mr. Summers contemplates severing his connection with the Wheatland country at the end of this season, as everything, I was disposed to think, pointed to his long connection with the country. Perhaps Borderer's advice unasked would be superfluous; therefore he refrains from giving it. Only hoping that "things are not what they seem."

FIFTEENTH WEEK, February 1st to the 6th.

When the history of the season of 1885-86 comes to be written it will be a tale of many bitter disappointments, more perhaps than any of its predecessors since 1854. Not a week has passed since the opening of the year without some postponed meets or dangerous attempts to combat the difficulties of the weather by hunting in some form. This has entailed much grief; its latest victim is poor Eli Skinner, than whom a more excellent whip never followed a pack, and it was a cruel fate that his horse should roll over on him in the snow on the side long ground about Wirsall on Sir Watkin's Hinton Wednesday. By the bye the Cloverley fox that gave them such an excellent run was, I find, killed at Shavington, not Cloverley as I stated, so that he more than completed his big ring before succumbing to the exigences of the occasion. I am told that the hounds fairly out-ran the horsemen over the flying country between Kent's Rough, Ash, and Cloverley—a thing rarely seen here, where such a never-to-be denied field had no excuse to offer for not being at least within a field of those flying sterns.

On Saturday, Sir Watkin hunted under difficulties at Oteley, the going being so bad that a friend of mine, who travelled there by rail, deemed discretion the better part of valour, and returned without his fun, so I have not been able to catch anything of their doings, and am obliged to say the same of the Halston Monday. Had there been any good sport, however, I think I should have heard of it.

It is a subject of universal regret in North Shropshire that Lady Frances Lloyd, the wife of Colonel R. Lloyd, of Aston, should have been so suddenly taken away, leaving a large family of ten children to mourn her loss. In every walk of life, no old Shropshire family is more respected than the Lloyds of Aston; and none are more devoted to the hunting field.

The Shropshire met at Loppington on Monday, on the boundary of their country between Wem and Ellesmere. This is always looked upon as an uncertain find, and the second draw at Broughton Gorse is often the speculative rendezvous of a portion of the field hailing Shrewsbury way. To-day, this clever division were doomed to disappointment. A fox was at home at Loppington that proved a good one. The country that he chose was negotiable, but bristling with obstacles, towards Petton in Sir Watkin's country, then circling to Slape Gorse, and, continuing the wheel, leaving Wem on his right, they checked near Horton. This nice gallop appeared to have come to an end when up jumped the hunted fox, that had been taking a brief rest, and away they went again to Loppington, and over a similar line to that of starting, finishing up near Loppington with a pretty kill. Thus a very enjoyable run of about two hours was chronicled with jumping enough for the veriest glutton. In the afternoon, contrary to custom, and much to the annoyance of many, Broughton Gorse was not the afternoon draw, and a long trot was taken to Soulton, where a fox took them to Weston Heath to ground.

On Wednesday, attractions were divided between Hinton, close to Whitchurch, with Sir Watkin, or Condover Hall, with the Shropshire. To show the varieties of our fickle climate, snowstorms at Hinton almost prevented hunting, while south of the Severn all was *en règle*, if we set aside a drizzling rain. It carried us back to days of yore, when Smith Owen was the backbone of hunting in Shropshire, to see the hounds once again gathered in front of this fine old place, and, more than all, to see such a goodly company in attendance. This is the first meet for the last three or four years that has taken place at Condover. Foxes now, however, are once more preserved, and the new occupier, Mr. Close, is to be congratulated on his sportsmanlike conduct.

Bomere having been disturbed on Wednesday, and the lying in the park being cut down a good deal by the weather, no fox turned up till Cantlop was reached. Here there was a quick find, and as quick a scamper away towards Pitchford to the Oak, but, without crossing the main road, he turned left-handed to Bourton, as if for Bomere; not liking the water, however, he turned up by the side of the brook, past the Green, into Condover Park, where he managed to elude the hounds, probably going to ground in a drain there, which had sufficient water in it to make a terrier decline closer acquaintance with it. A fast twenty minutes. Pitchford big wood held a fox, but thanks to the bad behaviour of some of the field, who were three-parts through it before hounds entered (it is no use preaching to them), he stole away, and was seen to enter the gardens, where terriers up and down trees, and various kinds of ferreting, failed to put him out. Golding Coppice held a brace, one of which got nailed in covert, and the other went away to Eaton Mascott, and was there lost. A not very satisfactory day.

Things again looked blue in their hunting aspect for the rest of the week. Haughmond Abbey was a failure, which was a universal disappointment, seeing that hounds have not been into Holly Coppice since October, probably an unprecedented event, and one that does not please the sporting associations of Sundorne Castle.

On Saturday, in worse frost, if anything, than the day before, the Shropshire essayed a bye day at Shawbury, found a fox, and ran him to ground, when the rest of the day was profitably (?) expended in digging him out.

I dare say they will hunt to-day at Baschurch, but Borderer doubts the wisdom or pleasure of trusting valuable horses (or their riders either) to do their best while there is an unmistakeable bone in the air.

Rumours are unusually rife of the retirement of masters of hounds. I have already alluded to one which is threatened in Shropshire, but which I hope will not be carried out. There is another retirement, however, that comes with a heavy thud upon South Shropshire. Mr. C. W. Wicksted has for more than twenty years guided the destinies of the Ludlow country, and in his hands one of the most beauteous pack of hounds, full of the choicest blood that English kennels and long practical experience and good judgment could bring together, has been maintained. The inheritance of a famous hunting name from the country of Woore was not an empty phrase with Mr. Wicksted, for if ever a thorough love of sport in all its branches was endued by inheritance on man, so certainly its example is the present Master of the Ludlow, who is now about to give up the reins of government to, I believe, a young and worthy successor. Of this I would speak on a future occasion. Your space will not permit me to enter as fully as I would wish into the glories and successes of that tight little hunt, the Ludlow, for the last twenty-five years. I could recount many and many a splendid run in which I have participated with them, and it is a pleasure seldom witnessed so strongly elsewhere to ese the master's triumphs so genuinely entered into by one and all who are there.

There you never hear of quarrels, coverts closed against the masters, jealousies, or bickerings. Whether people are less hard to please there than elsewhere Borderer knows not, but they are pleased, and no one for one moment doubts that the best energies of a master's life are there centred on showing sport from one end of his country to the other. It will be only when the separation comes in its cruel reality that the Ludlow men will realise their loss. How truly the lines written of his father, by Warburton, come back to us as we picture the son :—

> When scent on the fallow is failing,
>   Should a check from o'er riding ensue ;
> Hear Charlie the mischief bewailing,
>   With sorrow so touching and true.
>
> Whoo-hoop ! There's an end of the scurry.
>   Now Charley with might and with main.
> First dances, then shouts " Worry ! worry !"
>   Then shouts and then dances again.
>
> While I've health to go hunting with Charley,
>   I envy no monarch his crown.

SIXTEENTH WEEK, February 8th to the 13th.

The full programme of Shrewsbury Spring Races and Steeplechases is now out, and I hope will receive due attention, so that when the 8th and 9th of April come round, sport will be in the ascendant.

I had intended some copious notes on the Grand National, but my hunting jottings this week demanded so much attention that I must forego the subject until nearer the day of the race, merely remarking that I like the looks of Redpath, Azuline, Ringlet, Ivanhoe, Gerona, Saveyard, and Sinbad.

In hunting, as in other things, history repeats itself, and it is refreshing to take a peep backwards, and see what "Nimrod" had to tell us of Shropshire doings in 1850, and find the scene of sport, as well as the chief actors therein, have changed so little. Here are a couple of days in a week then to compare with those of last week :—

"On the following day the fixture was at Acton Burnell, the seat of the well-known sportsman, Sir Edward Smythe, where foxes, good cheer, ale, and hospitality invariably abound. As a matter of course, they soon found in the park, but the fox went to ground in a rabbit spout, where he was left to his meditations. Found again at Frodesley Hill, had a pretty burst of twenty minutes' duration, and again to ground at Acton Burnell. The grand event, however, is now to be recorded. They met at the fifth milestone on the Baschurch Road. The hounds were scarcely in the covert, at Merrington, which belongs to Mr. Slaney, one of the members for Shrewsbury, a most zealous sportsman, when the fox was viewed away by Pearce, the head whip. After taking a ring round the covert he pointed his head for Leaton Shelf, best pace. Without a moment's hesitation he ran through the covert as straight as possible to Preston Gobalds, and away to Pimhill, Harmer Hill, and Middle Park, nearly to Baschurch. Still bearing to the left, he regained the covert in which he was found at Merrington. Through it again to Leaton Shelf; he then crossed the river Severn, which, although bank full, Mr. Webster, of Preen, plunged into, leaving the whole field behind him. This was, however, an unprofitable daring, for, having tried a refuge in Bickley Coppice, the fox re-crossed the Severn near Montford Bridge, which afforded Mr. Webster another opportunity for exercising his amphibious qualities.

"From this point to Forton, and nearly to Nesscliffe; here he turned to the right by Fitz, with the pack close at his brush; through the gardens at Grafton, when he once more tried the earths at Leaton Shelf, and after a terrific run of nearly four hours, he was run into near Leaton Knoll, the residence of J. A. Lloyd, Esq., a small portion only of the field being up to witness the termination; but of the select few were Mr. Baker, the present, and Mr. Eyton, the late master of these hounds, Mr. Webster, and Mr. Harnage. Although not up at the finish, Mr. Lloyd, of Aston, went remarkably well; but all the horses were completely beaten, and had it not been for some friendly road which occasionally intervened, it appears impossible that any could have gone half way."

On Tuesday the South Cheshire had a good meet; but Borderer was bound for South Shropshire to have a peep at very old friends in the Ludlow country. Onibury Station lay handy and tempting, with an excellent mount awaiting him. How could he resist? An uninviting morning—cold, misty, and cheerless—and yet there are elements in the hunting field which defy such drawbacks as these, and we soon forget them. The hills to-day were a mixture of fog and snow, with an unexhausted frost in the ground, that made a move into a lower atmosphere imperative. Cookeridge is a splendid covert, but it seldom brings luck, and to-day there was little hope, because it had been disturbed only last week. The decoy, too, seldom fails, but here again the same excuse was forthcoming. A fox had been on the move in the covert overhanging the river in anticipation of a visit from the hounds, so that, beyond hunting his stale line, no fun resulted here. There was nothing for it but a peregrination to Ferney Dingles, where the Master soon put us on the *qui vive* by a view halloa on the Marlow top ground. Hounds did not come very quickly, but hunted prettily to the Kennel Dingle, where the fox made a very queer double, and then went back to Ferney; and we buried ourselves in a dismal fog as he again crossed the high ground into the Limekiln Wood and Mocktree Hayes. Snow lay deep at the hedges, and jumping was decidedly dangerous. A fresh fox was viewed away here, and we crossed the main road in good style for Hargrove to Cophall, and so on slowly to Downton Walks, where a dodging fox and a touchy scent combined to bringing our hunting to an end. It was not a day to see the Ludlow at their best, but nobody could be displeased with the way the hounds did their work. So much music and close hunting in the bitch pack I never saw. The dogs are Wicksted's favourites, and always have been. Better luck will I trust, favour me if I chance upon another day with them ere the season closes. Some nice young horses I saw in the field to-day in the hands of farmers should not be lost sight of. It is sad indeed to think that this is to be the Master's last season, after twenty years unexampled success. What the Ludlow country will be without Wicksted I dare not think, for he has indeed shown himself to be a first-rate sportsman. There are rumours of a successor, but nothing authentic is known as yet. You shall hear more anon.

The Cheshire Tuesday, I hear, was a good one, but not having been present I cannot give particulars.

On Wednesday the Shropshire met at Acton Burnell, the grand old seat of Sir Frederick Smythe, Bart., so full of historic interest. The morning was frosty but the low ground rode well, so that a fair muster turned up, including a few North Shropshire worthies. The Park Wood was left in peace, and the Holly Wood and the Obelisk were foxless. Pitchford has had very frequent calls made upon it this year, but never in vain, I am delighted to say. Colonel Cotes has indeed shown a splendid example of fox preservation this year. A brace were going to-day in no time, the hounds settling on the vixen, and she ran at once into the home drain. Her companion, however, had in the meantime been viewed away at the top of the covert, and Thatcher at once galloped to the scene of his departure, where, despite his ten minutes' start they dashed away grandly across the Frodesley Road, and over a pleasant line to Ryton, where a left-handed turn soon brought his pursuers to Longnor. He did not, however, enter the wood here, but went on to the foot of the Lawley, where hounds threw up. This had been the cream of the thing—nice jumping fences, plenty of them, and the pace just sociable enough for the majority to enjoy the fun. I grieve to say that the Master, Mr. Lonsdale, came down with a nasty thud on landing into a road, horse and all, and it was a great relief to see him able to get into the saddle again and continue the chase. Thatcher hit off his fox cleverley to Frodesley Hill, and slowly down to Pitchford again, where he ran them out of scent—a very pretty hunting run. The first fox had wisely quitted the drain, and so after an *al fresco* luncheon at the hall,

Golding's Coppice, which produced a brace last week, was tried. Here they were again, and the right one being the chosen one of the pack this time, they rattled away merrily down the brook side, not crossing until approaching Cound, by the Iron Bridge, and leaving Eaton Mascot on his left, ran parallel with the railway up to the level crossing opposite Cross Houses. Here an unfortunate check ensued, and Thatcher held them over the line, whereas the fox had declined crossing. Thanks to a holding scent, on they went again until, nearing Berrington, the fox crossed the line, when Thatcher had made up his mind that Bomere was his point. A holloa brought him back, and hounds again hunted prettily to Chilton, where, in the bank at the back of the house, in poor Harry Burton's favourite earth, he made himself safe, after giving them a very nice hunting run over a good and rather unusual line. Great were the stories of grief and deeds of daring that had taken place during the day—a daring M.D. jumping the wire fence that runs parallel with Eaton Mascot drive. Others charged iron rails unintentionally, and came safely out of the encounter. Young men and horses were hung up in hairy fences, and caught in the ditches beyond; in fact, dirty coats were the order of the day, all, however, harmless and happy in their results.

Amid the varying attractions of the week a peep into Radnorshire could not be resisted. A telegram on Thursday reported frost really going and hunting certainly possible. An early start, thirty miles by train, and a four mile drive before breakfast, sharpens the appetite—a couple of miles jog, and I am at Pilleth, in the pretty Lugg Valley, where every field recalls a pleasant memory. Such a bright beautiful morning, too, with the snow on the high ground, adding vigour to the landscape and making a sportsman's heart leap at the idea of coming events. Those hounds, too, seem to add their welcome to one now almost a stranger to them. Had they quite forgotten me? In a moment of unpardonable conceit, I thought they had not, as they looked up with wagging sterns, and their countenances brimful of sense, clustering round an old friend. Comparisons are not always favourable, but here I looked over once more those fine backs and loins, iron limbs, and sensible countenances, for which the Welsh cross in hounds is famous, and I was proud of having been so long a sharer in their fortunes. Their like are hard to find. Our field is select, but one and all with their hearts in the sport, more pinks than blacks, and the Colonel looking as fresh and young as he did ten years ago. Nantygroes Wood is our first venture, and the home of a brace. We try conclusions with the wrong one, that is not keen for a start, and as the orders are not to let him go up country into the snow if possible, and no other way is pleasing to him, after two or three turns he falls a victim. Ganders Bridge Gorse lies in high latitudes, but thither we go full of expectation, and sure enough it is brimful of foxes, at least half-a-dozen going away in different directions. We manage to get about eleven couple on the back of one, and he goes away in view a cracker over the top, and down into Treburvah Dingle towards the Blancwm. Now turning to the right over Gwernaffel big enclosures it is hard galloping to Cwmblowen, where hounds check, and we hear another pack on the opposite hill towards Pilleth. The Colonel puts on the steam, and we are soon with them by Pilleth Church and along the side of the hill towards Monaughty, there dropping down, we cross the road and over the Lugg. Disdaining the shelter of the Forest Wood, this good fox goes on by Upper Litton and over Litton Hill, beating us in good style in the bright sunshine of midday. Henewm Gorse fails to hold one, but Norton is no sooner reached than away we are again with evidently three or four on foot. Luckily, however, by the time we cross the Presteign and Knighton Road at Hares' Green, we have the pack with us and push on to Black Patch, where it is evident that we have a brace of foxes before us—the lines run curiously parallel now in the same field, now crossing each other, and as we reach the Stone Wall hill converging quick volunteer whips put all to rights, and we sail away as hard as hoofs can carry us to Willey Wood. Yonder goes a fox over the top of Hill Pike— not our hunted one, for there is a full chorus back in the covert—no peace for him here, he tries a turn in the open, but is obliged to retrace his steps, and at last slips away by Stocking Farm and Wood, to the Colony, where we have some slow hunting into the Farm Wood. In the meantime a couple-and-a-half of hounds have brought another fox by another route to meet us, and I think our hunted fox's life is spared, as we join forces after the new comer. It is serious work for the horses, as on we go back through the Willey Coverts and down towards Presteign, skirting the cemetery, right into Boullibrooke grounds, through the stableyard, and on to Norton Mill, then right handed over the road into the park at Norton, where he keeps the lower ground until at the Ackhill end he turns up to the Long Wood, and it is a race for life by the Old Manor House, and, over on the new road above the Moors, to ground in a rabbit hole, just in front of them. It is half-past five, and we have been running hard since half-past two. The hounds deserve him, and by six o'clock they have him—thus winding up the most sporting and enjoyable day possible, as it should be, with legitimate blood. To say that Borderer was charmed with the way hounds did their work is not doing justice to his feelings. He, once more for the one-hundredth time, reiterates his opinion that there is nothing in the hound creation to beat a judicious cross of the high-bred English foxhound with the true and equally pure-bred Welsh hound—well kennelled and well disciplined " they lick creation " in the shape of foxdom. Why more M.F.H's, do not try to cross is more than I can understand, seeing how many packs nowadays suffer from lack of nose, as well as tongue and drive. There are few packs that have been brought to such a state of perfection in this respect, thanks to the untiring devotion of Colonel Price for the last fifteen years, than have the Radnorshire and West Hereford.

Nearer home the sun shone with almost summer brightness on the Shropshire at the fifth milestone on the Baschurch Road. Business did not begin very quickly, in expectancy of the Master's coming. Fitz Coppice held a fox, which the field appeared to think had gone away on the Walford side long before he had any thoughts of doing so, and several fences were unnecessarily jumped. All he really did was to dodge back to the church, and go to ground near the river. A brace in the Shelf yielded hardly any fun. There was a fox in Hencote Pool that

some thought was lame, but he proved too nimble for the hounds with the poor scent forthcoming to-day, and made a safe retreat towards Berwick and on to Leaton Lodge, his whereabouts being traceable no further. In the evening a good thing came off for the few left to enjoy it. Merrington to Middle Park Church, Harmer Hill and Pimhill, then by Merrington Green to the place of departure, and on Bomere Heath to Leaton at nightfall.

Saturday was productive of better things, a truer hunting morning never dawned, and Mr. Frank Bibby is ever keen to show what Hardwicke can produce in the way of foxes. His gorse has never failed this season, and now it held a regular straight backed one that waved his brush boldly to his foes, and was off like a shot towards Harmer Hill, then bending to right did not touch Broughton Gorse or Shingler's, and kept a capital line. The racing pace had told its inevitable tale on the long line of horsemen that spread over the landscape. A check here brought people together, and at a slower pace they hunted on past Burlton Mill, and nearly to Petton, where he was given up. A good straight seven mile point. Back to Shingler's Gorse, hard by, when up jumped number two, also a straight chap, for he took them over the London and North Western Railway at a great pace, and never halted until he reached Grinshill when a plethora of foxes confused matters for a time, until Thatcher succeeded in accounting for one or other of its denizens. Whether Broughton Gorse gave an evening gallop or not a one-horse man could not say. Be this as it may, however, the day was a good one, and will rank among the best of the season, both for pace and country.

Is it not time that a meeting was called to decide on what shall be done about the South Country next season? There seems little or no desire for separation now, but public opinion is always worth gauging.

SEVENTEENTH WEEK, February 15th to the 20th.

An unbroken week, such as the last, is an event in a winter such as this in our neighbourhood. Albeit Sir Watkin, when he left Ruabon by train for Baschurch, on Monday morning, must have had grave misgivings about the state of the ground, as it had frozen desperately on Sunday night, a large field turned up, and it was impossible to disappoint them, so, after an hour's grace, and thanks to the wind turning south-easterly, a move was made to Stanwardine Gorse. Its dark recesses had not been entered by a single hound ere an early caller from a distance had heard the rattle of hoofs, and the clamour of tongues up the approaching field, and he was off in hot haste on the far side with his nose for Petton. Lockey's chance was a good one, and so was the good doctor's, for while the former was galloping to clap them on his line, the latter was putting on the steam, just to remind the traveller that there was a better line open to him than Petton Shrubberies, and he took the hint gallantly. Straight as a crow would fly, by Stanwardine Hall he went, and the state of the ground had soon to be forgotten if you wanted to be near the head of affairs to-day. On to Kenwick, where people averred he was in the same field with the hounds. Anyhow he had plenty of spurt left in him, for there was no symptom of a turn. On over Tetch Hill, leaving the Lea Woods on his right, almost to Frankton, until he found an open earth at Hardwick, near Ellesmere. A straight six miles in thirty-five minutes, the country good, and everyone had to do his best. What more could have been desired? I will refrain from multiplying or enlarging upon the grief—suffice it to say that the kick was taken out of the horses, and few one-horse men cared to endorse a second attack on Petton after a long jog back there, especially as hounds again went away hotly from the Marton Plantations and taking an exactly opposite line to that of the morning, went by Marton, just missing the boggy ground, crossed the G.W.R. to Walford, and marked their fox to ground between their and Leaton, as far as I can make out. Grumblers have nothing to say against such a day as this.

On Tuesday, Mr. Corbet was not favoured with such a good scent with which to amuse his multitude of followers. Major Starkey's gorse put forth the first fox, which was lost at Hadley Park. Quoisley provided No. 2, but this is not a favourite spot for the thrusters, as there are two or three bottomless ditches that the farmer at Quoisley tells me generally cause an unhooking of his team at plough, "just to give 'em a help out," whenever Mr. Corbet comes this way. From here, the fox seems to have meandered about the Hinton coverts, then by Peel's Gorse to Marbury and Osmere, eventually being lost just beyond, on the Whitchurch side, the whole run being an invasion of Sir Watkin's territory.

Wednesday had a variety of attractions. Carden stood first in the affections of the majority, and right well they were rewarded by a sharp scurry in the morning nearly to the Duckington Hills, interspersed with watery episodes that added sauce to the repast. In the afternoon, a long hunting run of two hours from near Edge all over the Broughton country, very difficult to describe, and still more to decipher on the map, in which I believe Lockey showed great patience and wisdom, but was not rewarded by a kill.

Montford Bridge with the Shropshire on the identical Wednesday was not so fashionable. Nevertheless, its chronicle is no mean one—a brace in Bickley Wood— the hounds settled on the wrong one, who after being headed, made a short peregrination to the Isle and back, and eventually got to ground. The dog fox, meanwhile, had crossed the river. Preston Rough was tenantless, but Gough's Coppice is generally a lucky little place, and to-day was no exception. Some eager starters on the road nearly spoilt the fun, but he only skirted the wood again and was off, leaving Cardiston on his left, to Woodcote and Cruckton Pool at a capital pace. A sharp turn here over the railway brought difficulties, but there was a holloa forward Onslow way, and over the main road he had been viewed, but Thatcher's darlings could barely own his line to Bickley, and he lives to fight another day. Trotting back, a third main was thrown directly the hounds reached Onslow Withy Bed. A good wild fox did not wait to be found ere he was off, and a very nice run he afforded. Going by Onslow House (all thanks to Col. Winfield for our find), he crossed the main road to Calcot, and leaving Preston Montford on his right crossed the Holyhead Road for Bickley. Swinging, however, to the right, he did not touch the wood, skirted the road down to the Isle, recrossed the Holyhead Road near Oxton, and took them a nice line of grass with pretty jumpable fences, leaving Bicton on his left, until he eventually landed his pursuers in a hopeless check close to Hanwood Station, after giving them an exceedingly pretty hunting run of an hour, over as nice a line as there is in the county. The man in the balloon says that had Thatcher crowded on sail a little more to have helped his hounds at the critical moment, the fox would not have beaten them. He does not ride in the South Country with as much nerve and determination as he does near home. The run was not without a serious *contretemps*, which mercifully ended only in an awful looking fall. At Calcot, a frightful mantrap in the shape of a strand of wire had been run through a very tempting looking fence, without any notification of its presence whatever. Mr. George Butler Lloyd, our respected secretary of the South Country, and banker, charged it in full swing, and his horse was caught like a rabbit, rolling over him twice. How he escaped seemed a marvel to those who stood shuddering on the other side.

On Thursday, the Albrighton, at Gnosall, had unwonted disappointment—a late start. The Ranton Coverts blank; a Blakemere Pool fox was no sooner found than he was underground. Offley Grove, in the evening, my informant knows not of.

On Friday, at Shawbury White Gates, foxes did not turn up till they got to Lea Wood, where one was found, and quickly went to ground. In a pit hole close to the kennels, however, a better specimen made his appearance and like a shot out of a gun the hounds chevied him to Preston Springs, and out again on the Wem side to Palmers Hill, and Trench Farm, at a capital pace. The old grey was once more conspicuous in front, and a black coat playing a very good second fiddle. Here the fox turned up to the left, skirting Clive and Grinshill, only getting back to Lea Wood to be caught, after an exceedingly pretty ring that those in a good place enjoyed, and those behind wished themselves anywhere else. A good sportsman, hailing from the county town way, tried the depth of a nasty ditch, and it looked as if the grey mare came out of the encounter badly. I trust she may soon be all right again.

On Saturday, Sir Watkin spent his New Street Lane morning between Styche, Shavington, and Cloverley, killing a brace of bad foxes, and having very little real fun. In the evening, however, from Ash a fox took them a pretty gallop to Burley Dam and Lord Hopetown's Gorse, a line that needs no paint from me. Had it come earlier in the day it would have been more universally enjoyed.

Cressage Park with the Shropshire was a red letter day, for an account of which I am indebted to a friend who knows the country and has faithfully described it: "On Saturday, the 20th, the Shropshire met at Cressage, and a move was made for Bannister, which proved blank. Cressage Park was then drawn, and as foxes have been seen there for several weeks past we expected a run, but failed to find. We then drew through Lords Coppice and went away to Kenley Gorse, which was said to hold a brace; the cover is very thick, but after a long time in cover a fox was found and made for the Acton Burnell corner of the wood, where he was headed back and killed in cover. We then drew a nice piece of gorse at the Cressage end of Kenley Coppice, where a fox was found. He got a good start and went for the high ground between Acton Burnell and the Grange Hill, where he turned, choosing the Grange Hill route, and, after going two miles, he ran to ground in a drain on the flat on Mr. Munslow's farm. We then trotted on to the Hayes Coppice between Harnage Grange and Cressage, where we hoped to find the Cressage Park foxes, but they were not at home. The next order was Stevens Hill, where a stout one was found. He pointed for Harnage, but on leaving cover he made for the four turnings below Harnage Grange, where he again moved his point straight across Mr. Preece's farm, then over Mr. Heap's ground, past the Leasowes, then over the railway on to Mr. Pinkney's farm, and through the river Severn, leaving most of the field on the bank, one mile above Cressage Bridge; the hounds then went straight up the Eyton meadows for half a mile, when they turned and again crossed the river, three hundred yards above the old ferry, better known as the Punch Bowl Inn; the hounds came straight up to the railway, when the half-past three train from Shrewsbury was passing, but three or four of the field got between the hounds and the train, and saved the pack. We then hit off his line, up the Severn meadows to Cound Brickyard, where a check delayed us, but a friendly holloa at Venus Bank enabled our amateur huntsman and whips to get on this good fox again. The hunt servants were left sorrowing on the river brink, and were probably not aware that the hounds had re-crossed the river. The fox was now seen in the cover at the back of Venus Bank. He wished to make Eaton Mascot his point, but was headed back by a man on foot. We now expected to kill him in cover, but were mistaken, for he crossed the Blacksmith's Garden, where he was seen by the field a hundred yards in front of the pack, and then crossed the road and into the Long Dole Cover. The field went under the railway at the Brickyard, and away we went merrily for Brompton, and eventually lost all trace of the fox on the ploughed ground opposite Mr. Bather's house, at Wroxeter. The hounds cast forward up the river side past the mouth of the river Tern. On reaching the bend of the river, where the salmon are landed by the net fishers, the hounds crossed the river for the third time, leaving a small field of fifteen on the bank. On landing they could not hit off a line. Fortunately Thatcher appeared on the opposite bank just in time to take charge of the hounds, and would no doubt read in their countenances a full report of the run. The hounds lost the fox at about a quarter-past four, and were running about one hour and a half. There was plenty of fencing most of the way, and some very big jumping in the Severn meadows below Cound. All the field except about twenty, were thrown out at the river below the Punch Bowl. Mr. Hulton-Harrop made an excellent huntsman, and with one from Stapleton cut out most of the work. A little black mare from Harnage, a daring M.D. and a steeplechase horse from beyond the Edge

CAPTAIN AMES.

Wood, at times showed well to the front. We are glad to report that the South Shropshire gentlemen kept in the saddle better than they did last week." Surely after all the sport in the south this year, and while the season is yet in its prime, it would be wise to call a meeting to consider the future of this country. Borderer is not inspired, nor a prophet, but he believes it only needs a uniform promise of support to Mr. Lonsdale, and a truthful exposition of want of funds, to win from him the promise of putting, for next season, both the north and south countries on an equal footing, and to handsomely waive a subscription. If this were so, I believe there would be more heart thrown into hunting south of the river than we have seen for many a day, and that at least three new gorse coverts would be planted and tended with increasing care. " Hunting men of the south, do not let the grass grow under your feet. *Carpe diem*, and keep your hunting."

EIGHTEENTH WEEK, FEBRUARY 22ND TO THE 27TH.

If ever hunting men have been tried in the matter of weather, this Anno Domini, 1886, will stand out pre-eminently in this respect. I can recall no parallel since 1854, when the frost did not disappear before the end of the first week in March. Extraordinary, however, has been the scent, notwithstanding the bitter east wind, especially on the grass. Borderer always gives the foxes credit for favouring us a little through this amiable month of February in the matter of scent, and he believes as a physiological fact this is true.

Be this as it may, some very bright gems in way of sport have come to hand within the last week or two. Conspicuous amongst them being a great Worcestershire day on Lord Hindlip's birthday, who is so well known as Sir Henry Allsopp, that some of my readers will hardly recognise him under his new title. It has been an annual custom to meet at Hindlip on Sir Henry's birthday, and drink a bumper to foxhunting. On this occasion an unusual crowd of sportsmen came from far and wide; at least two hundred sat down to breakfast, and nearly four hundred mustered in the field. The run from Goose Hill was so remarkable that it deserves to be chronicled in the annals of Worcestershire hunting. I have been fortunate in obtaining a thoroughly reliable, and in every way correct account of it from end to end, for which I plead no excuse in giving in the author's own words. It is no exaggeration to say that not a tithe of the starters saw the end, or that the Crowle Brook never had so many winter bathers in its muddy waters within living memory. Nor has the old Crowle steeple-chase course been the scene of such genuine fun for many a long year. How proud Mr. Ames must feel over this ever memorable Hindlip day! "Friday, February 19th, the Worcestershire Hounds met at Hindlip. A vast crowd assembled to greet Lord Hindlip. The small coverts in the park contained no fox, so a move was made to Oakley Wood, which was also blank, and Hazlewood was equally unfortunate. Goosehill next claimed attention, and though the hounds were twice in it on the 15th, two foxes were on foot as soon as the hounds entered this fine wood, of which Mr. Bearcroft may be as proud as of his beautiful old hall of the seventeenth century. Both foxes broke on the Hanbury side. The hounds ran to the Church laurels, then round the north side of the park, crossing at the end of the deer park, and disturbing another fox in the belt (Hanbury is full of foxes.) Denton went on with the fox he had been running all the time, but several couples of hounds followed the lately-disturbed fox. The hunted fox ran over Hunting-trap Farm, leaving Goosehill close on his left, straight to the Trenches, through it, and ran the beautiful grass meadows on the other side of Crowle Brook to below Crowle Thrift, where he crossed but did not go to the Thrift, preferring to go down wind, thus leaving Churchill Wood close on the left, he went to Spetchley station, then straight on down the flat for Botany Bay, when a fresh fox jumped up, some distance behind the pack, who were too intent upon the fox before them to notice all the shouting from the railway and elsewhere after the fresh fox. The hunted fox held on as if for the turnpike road for Stoulton, but left it on his right and ran on by Wolverton's farm, crossing the railway near Hand's Brake and the Pershore turnpike road, into Mr. Whittaker Wilson's park. He was run into there. When taken from the hounds, he stood as if he had not a joint in his body. Time, one hour, fifty minutes, distance from Hanbury Church to Caldwell, eleven and half miles on the ordnance map, to which must be added the distance from Goosehill to Hanbury, and allowance for deviations would make some sixteen to seventeen miles. Unfortunately the brooks and the pace, though a very fine flat line and mostly grass, allowed but a few to see this real good fox eaten at ten minutes to four."

Monday took Sir Watkin to Iscoyd, where he scored wonderfully, in fact eclipsed all his previous good Mondays in the eyes of many. Here, again, I am fortunate in having a friendly author, who permits me to quote him:—

"Sir W. W. Wynn's hounds, at Iscoyd, Tuesday, 23rd inst., found several foxes in the snug cover at the bottom of the Park, got away with one, and ran him through the Bubney Dingles, and out up the valley, right into the town of Whitchurch, the fox taking refuge amongst the shrubs in Dr. Nottingham's garden. However the hounds soon routed him out, and killed him in front of the doctor's house. No. 2 was in waiting in the same cover, but he simply went about fifty yards and to ground in a drain. I regret to say that about this time poor Skinner, the much-respected first whip, met with an extraordinary accident. As I am informed, he was leading his horse and carrying a terrier. For some reason the horse got restive, and struck at the terrier with his fore foot, and in doing so struck Skinner on the face. The blow was a nasty one, but what was the exact state of the injury I have not heard. Failing to dislodge this rat of a fox, the hounds were taken to the Kiln Green Wood. They found directly, and the fox lost no time in getting away. He broke at the Wyches End, and ran straight into Scholars' Wood, through which he ran without dwelling. Binding to the right, he ran past Chidlow, over the Whitchurch and Chester Railway, and on past Chad Church, leaving Macefen

Gorse about two fields to the left, over the boggy Willy Moor Meadows to Bar Mere. Here we came to a check, the fox having evidently run up the road some distance towards Cholmondeley; for on Lockey casting in that direction he hit off the line, and a moment afterwards our fox was viewed; therefore, getting on good terms with him again, the hounds pressed him on through Norbury Common, and out on the far side as if pointing for Wrenbury Mosses; but after going a few fields he turned to the left, and running a ring, pushed his way into Cholmondeley, close to the Home Farm, and on through Bretts Moss (the most foxy cover in all Cheshire). Whether we changed here or not I cannot say, but it is most likely we did, for hounds were quickly away on the far side, and ran at a very good pace straight up to Hampton. Here they checked for a moment or two close to a farm yard, the fox having evidently been headed, for he turned to the left and set his head straight for the Larkton Hills, but most extraordinary to relate, when just within one field of the hills, he turned to the left, and ran past Duckington, leaving the wood of that name close to the right, over the Chester Road, through the Hooks plantation, and on to below Carden Lodge, the scent getting cold. I hear that Lockey at this stage whipped off the hounds. I, myself, left them by the Hooks plantation, having a long ride home before me. I believe the time was about two and a half hours. Up the Larkton there was nothing to complain about as to pace, for the hounds kept plodding steadily on. Most of the line is stiffish, and some parts were very happy, and I regret to hear that Captain Paley broke the back of as good a hunter as ever looked through a bridle. Another well-known retired officer emerged from the bottom of a ditch bootless, his gee kindly performing the part of boot jack, whilst his jovial valet *pro tem* of some fifteen stone weight, tugged away with all his might at his master's prostrate form. I hope that none of the actors are any the worse. Second horses were at a premium, as the line taken did not enable them to nick in."

On Wednesday at Stapleton Village, with the Shropshire, there was not sufficient frost to stop hounds. Of sport, however, I cannot write, because the required animal refused to turn up anywhere, although known to be about. Stapleton, Netley, Lythwood, Bomere, and Betton were requisitioned in vain—the first blank day of the season, I believe, and it is one, I am sure, that will be explained away before its close.

On Friday it looked as if the fixture at Mr. Sparrow's, of Albrighton Hall, could not be brought off. The ground was as hard as adamant at ten o'clock About noon, however, the sun broke out, and the elements relaxed their ferocity. Preston Gubbalds soon put the possibility of riding to the test, and people, who a few minutes before had been shaking their heads, and talking of going home, were seen pounding away for Hardwicke, and jumping fences, as if of frost there was none. Not crossing the road the fox made to the left to Pimhill, and out at the bottom for Merrington, where he gave them the slip. Birchy Moor was the next find, from whence a fox got away quickly towards Albrighton, then to the right, down to the railway by Leaton, and on towards the Moss, where there was a missing link between him and the pack, which could not be recovered. Hencote Pool then gave forth No. 3, that ran an exceedingly pretty ring over much the same ground as the last fellow, and eventually went to ground in the middle of a field near Hencote. The Gubbalds again were tried, and again was a fox on foot, that very soon went away for Pimhill. After going two fields, however, the pack met with another fox, that had jumped up out of a hedgerow in view, and him they caught very quickly—he being minus a leg, and as it turned out a regular hen-roost robber, that deserved his fate. The hunted fox, in the meantime, although viewed into Pimhill, had gone too far to be recovered. Would that a rather enjoyable, and decidedly foxy, day had ended here. Hardwicke Gorse was drawn, and a vixen chopped. This is hard lines on its good owner, who has shown a fox here, I think it is eight times this season. There was no blame to-day as to heading her, and so it must be put down entirely to the chapter of accidents.

On Saturday "King Nip" put down his foot so strongly, that hunting at Prees Heath was, I should say, quite impracticable, while, as I write, March is being ushered in by rude Boreas and snow, rendering the proverbial Baschurch Monday once more a delusion. Perhaps, after all, this snow is coming to clear off the remnant of its predecessors that still lingers on the hills, and that in a few days we shall be tasting the first delights of spring.

The land of Ludlow rejoices in that the reign of Wicksted is not to be cut short—his abdication having been withdrawn. The old Woore verses will still ring out with truth, and " We'll still go a hunting with Charlie."

Our local steeplechasing opens this week at Welshpool, that is if the awe-inspiring elements will sufficiently relent to enable what was last year a very stiff and badly laid outline to be negotiated safely. All the world goes to Welshpool, which is decidedly fun.

Do not forget, my foxhunting friends, about the meeting on Saturday to consider what shall be done about hunting the South country next season.

NINETEENTH WEEK, March 1st to the 6th.

The record has been beaten, and the Ides of March may prove more inexorable than living memory can recall. What folly it seems to head an article with " Horses and Hounds " when, like Othello, " their occupation is gone," and this detestable winter has made prisoners of hunting men for another long snowy and frost-bound week. To look forward with such a determined foe at our door is impossible, so the only alternative is to take a leaf out of the currant jelly book and cast back. Here I accidently hit on a pleasant bit of stale scent—a line written as far back as 1832, on the late Mr. Wicksted and the Woore country, and of Shropshire, which may beguile a few minutes now. My author says :—" On reaching Beteley, I was sorry to find Mr. Wicksted had been labouring under ill-health, from which, however, he is progressively recovering. He accompanied me to the kennels. A period of five or six years has elapsed since I saw this gentleman's hounds, and though report had repeatedly whispered their high character into my ear, yet my anticipated notions were much below the mark. I expected to see very fine hounds, but never for one moment suspected that the most beautiful pack in the world was about to pass in review before me. They had been fed about an hour before, and they consequently presented themselves under considerable disadvantage. When, however, the door was opened, I was very much surprised indeed—I was astonished; pleasingly so, certainly, for I had never seen a pack the *coup d'œil* of which threw such uniform beauty on the eye. If the *tout ensemble* was thus surprisingly interesting, the individual detail was more so. They are not the tallest hounds I have seen, they are about five-and-twenty inches in height, remarkable for bone, strength, and beautiful symmetry. The bitches appear as high as the dogs, and in consequence they exhibit a levelness which I never witnessed in any other pack. Beyond all question, I never saw hounds in such fine, such healthy, such perfect condition. These hounds unite the best blood in the kingdom, and their breeding and getting together have evidently been directed by the most acute perception, the most consummate judgment. The Rutland blood is a great favourite with Mr. Wicksted. I could not perceive anything like a middling or indifferently-formed hound—they were a collection of perfect beauties! Joker, a splendid dog, five years old, has received an injury upon his near thigh, which has wasted the limb, and incapacitated him from going out with the pack; yet, as a stallion, he is invaluable. His four two-year-old daughters (Carnage, Crafty, Crazy and Cruel), out of Countess (all at the same litter), are, taken either separately or collectively, very superior hounds; very beautiful, perfect! Mr. Wicksted was kind enough to indulge my curiosity for a considerable length of time, and drew out the hounds in various ways. At length I asked him if he could draw an indifferent hound —he smiled. They are short-legged hounds, possessing uncommon strength as well as uncommon beauty. I never before felt so much gratification from a view of hounds in the kennel, twenty three couple and a half.

"Mr. Wicksted, like Sir Richard Puleston, goes out five days in the fortnight. His country, (Staffordshire) appears to be one of considerable extent, and, although I am not altogether a stranger to it, I was not aware that it contained woodlands of 1,015 acres, and these woodlands, which ought to produce many cubs yearly, I was sorry to find, seldom held a single litter. Fox stealers abound in these parts, and Mr. Wicksted remarked that if the snow should fall, so as to enable the fox stealers to trace, all the foxes in these (the remoter) parts of his country would be taken. Who are the purchasers of these foxes? 'If there were no receivers of stolen goods there would be no thieves.'

"Shropshire, as a hunting country, I found like all other hunting countries, after much rain has fallen, deep and heavy. From the strong, rich quality of the soil, I should suppose it must, generally speaking, carry a good scent. Its aspect is different from that of Leicestershire, yet it pleased me better notwithstanding the strong impression which is uniformly felt for the spot where we first breathed the vital air, and the country which formed the scenes of early life. It so happened that the frost interfered very much with my excursion to Shropshire, and, what was still worse, when I went out with the hounds, very little sport was obtained. The hounds are very similar in appearance to those of Sir H. Mainwaring, as I have already observed, and are uncommonly well managed both in the kennel and in the field. Staples, the huntsman, is a philosopher in his way: reserved and civil, he is all attention to business; nor do I know which to admire most, his steady, cool, and quick method with his hounds, or the skill which he displays in the management of his horse. He served his apprenticeship under a great master, Sir Bellingham Graham, and is a credit to the school in which he acquired a very superior knowledge of his profession. He is well supported by two active clever whips. Independently of its prime home brewed (which is everywhere dispensed with so much good will) Shropshire, as a hunting country, stands pre-eminently conspicuous in one respect—such a thing as a surly, 'ill-tempered farmer is not to be met with; such a being could not exist here; he would be avoided as a pest, or driven from the country like a mad dog:—My ears were not stunned with the vociferation—' 'Ware wheat! 'Ware clover! 'Ware seeds!' so common in many other parts of England. In Shropshire, the farmers themselves are the first to set the example of riding over wheat.

"The Wrekin, which forms a conspicuous object from many situations in the neighbourhood of Shrewsbury, and which holds many foxes, is seldom, if ever, drawn. Foxes frequently make for this celebrated mountain, where they are given up. I was told that it is impossible to get foxes away from it: yet Tom Moody made them fly. It may surely answer the purpose of cub-hunting. Hawkstone is equally difficult, foxes will not leave it.

The most extraordinary run which has occured this season with the Shropshire hounds, took place in the early part of the month of December. The fixture was Ercall Mill. A fox was found in Pointon Springs, he was rattled through various coverts, and stood up before the hounds for two hours and a quarter, in which time he had led them across twenty five miles of country, a great part of which had been at a quick pace, when he contrived to get to ground, the leading hounds at his brush. The drain was of no great extent, and some of the hounds forced themselves into it at both ends; so that the fox was placed between two parties of his unsparing pursuers, and thus deprived of the power of moving either way, while the latter were unable to reach their object. Will Staples, the huntsman, began to move the earth with the end of his whip (the drain being superficial) while his whips were in quest of more effective instruments for the purpose. By the time a spade was procured, Staples had ascertained the exact position of the fox. He was immediately bolted, and not being able to run, sought shelter under the briars in the ditch. Staples instantly thrust his hands into the briars and seized the fox; but unluckily placing one hand by the side of the fox's head, and happening to have a crooked finger upon that hand—from some previous injury—which came laterally in contact with the fox's mouth, the latter got it between his grinders, where he held it almost as fast as if it had been screwed in a vice. In this situation, Staples drew the fox from the briars; and, as they did not part company, some of the gentlemen called to him to loose the fox.

"'He won't loose me,' cried Staples.

"In a second or two he dropped, and was instantly seized again by the unflinching huntsman, and thrown amongst the hounds. But as the usual ceremonies had not been performed, it became necessary to regain possession of the fox, which Staples was not able to effect, owing to the severe pain he felt, arising from the operation of the fox's teeth. The hounds, in an instant, deprived the fox of life, and he was taken from them by Mr. Clay; after undergoing the usual process, he was thrown a second time amongst the hungry pack, and quickly disappeared."

After this reminiscence, Borderer takes heart to make a for'ard cast beyond even the possibilities of resuming hunting this season for a few fleeting days into the Elysian fields of another season, and he congratulates the Shrewsbury country on having arranged for their unity with their hitherto more favoured northern neighbours, and having won from Mr. Lonsdale the promise of his hunting their country free of cost next season. I have no doubt that an adequate poultry and covert fund will be provided, and that foxes will be well preserved—as well as some new coverts laid down. If advice can be judiciously given on such a subject, I would say let gratitude be evidenced by promptitude in this matter—a fund *now* provided, and the lives of breeding vixens saved will do more for our future sport than adopting the more cockney and less satisfactory method of turning down tame cubs. I know which mode of procedure most pleases a master, and conduces to sport.—And so Mr. C. Wicksted after all is going to retire from the Ludlow country! It is sad to have to write it after the flicker of hope he gave us a few days back. But we now resign ourselves to the inevitable, and devoutly wish Sir William Curtis as happy and durable a reign as has smiled upon his predecessor.

TWENTIETH WEEK, MARCH 8TH TO 13TH.

It is only *vis inertiæ* that compels me use my pen this week. The poor creatures of my fancy still eat the bread of idleness, and I hardly know which are most worthy of our compassion—the animals or their masters. My almanac already tells me that fox-hunting has ceased, although the custom of modern sportmen has carried it furtively, but successfully, a little further into the budding month of April. Still there is really very little left to us of its *premier qualité*, and the dregs of the season look as far off being tasted as they did a fortnight ago. Even the poor birds have long ceased to whisper their thoughts of spring, and are dying of cold and want. All animal nature is struggling to counteract the severity of an unexampled winter and spring combined, which even human nature only can endure with pain. Postponements are the order of the day—everything is being adjourned to a more convenient season. Steeplechasing, as well as hunting and coursing, has gone to the wall. We grumbled at losing the Grand National Hunt Steeplechases this year for our new course at Shrewsbury. Now, the boot is on the other leg; and we thank our luck at having been spared the disappointment which is the lot of Yorkshire Malton. Bangor Steeplechases are fixed for April the 2nd, and the stakes close on the 22nd inst. Already sales of hunting studs are advertised apace. I see there is to be an important one at Whitchurch this week, and that Mr. Etches will have an unusually choice lot to offer, hunters from the studs of Captains Cook, Kennedy, and Cotton, as well as from those of Messrs. Horton, Wynne, Eyton, Masefield, Glynn, Drake, Peele Ethelston, the late Randolph Caldecott, the artist, and others. Here there will be some bargains to be picked up for those who have faith in the future, and pockets not quite empty. It is a grand time for setting our houses in order.

As I notified shortly last week, the Shropshire have not lost sight of their opportunity, and I hear on all sides of the gratitude which the south country feels at the generous way in which Mr. Lonsdale has come forward to hunt the whole country next season free of cost. In the matter of foxes, I have already ventured my advice that the stock now left should, if possible, be protected during the breeding season, and this can mainly be done by liberality with the poultry fund, and its being so announced without delay. Keepers must be kept on the right side. I attribute the increase of foxes in some places I could mention, to the lessening of game preservation. There is something inherently antagonistic between a gamekeeper and a fox. An old story, which illustrates what I mean, is worth repeating here. A gentleman who was an M.F.H. in the West of England, and who tried to act up to the motto, "Foxes as well as pheasants," had just engaged a new head keeper. The man came from a rather suspicious quarter, but was strictly enjoined not to destroy the foxes, and this he promised faithfully to obey. There were two litters that spring in the park, which were occasionally visited during the summer by the master. One day, as autumn was drawing on, he went, after a rainy night, to see whether the cubs could be padded near the earth, but no sign of them was to be found. This aroused his suspicion, but the keeper averred that they had moved to another earth. The underkeeper was ordered to make further search; he did so, and found two places where the earth was freshly moved, and on turning it up found a brace of beautifully healthy cubs—each had had a leg broken in a trap. These carcases were duly brought to the master. The head keeper was sent for, and told that there was some suspicion of unfair play having been going on with the foxes. The keeper was resolute. "If there had been any foul play it was unknown to him, for he would not allow such a shameful thing on any account. He had taken every possible care of them." The M.F.H. replied "I do not believe you." "What, me, sir? I'll take my oath I have not killed them," quoth the keeper. "Do you mean that?" rejoined his master. "Then take the book," holding out the testamentary Bible, which, as a magistrate, he always kept by him. The keeper took the book in his hand, when the gentleman said " Hold hard, my friend," and ringing the bell, in walked the footman with the two cubs as before arranged. It now became too hot for the delinquent, and he blurted out:—" Well, then, I did do it, and I could not help it, for it would be unnatural in me not to kill what I was brought up to do." Of course he got the sack, and the M.F.H. imbibed a salutary lesson, which he has handed down to us for the sake of sport, "Trust not your keepers."

And now about these new gorse coverts, which when made will be a great boon to the country, especially the one Wroxeter way, and the other near Lythwood. Having had a good deal of experience in both sowing and planting gorses, I may be allowed a few words of advice. I have tried both planting and sowing, and succeeded in both, but prefer the latter as the more certain of the two methods. Plough in April, and sow barley or oats, not a heavy crop: then sow the gorse seed broadcast, exactly as you would other seeds, such as clover or rye grass, and harrow it in. At harvest-time cut the grain pretty high up the straw, and the stubble will protect the young gorse, which is very tender the first year. Rabbits will damage it the first winter, and must be kept off. Afterwards they do good, as they keep it open under for foxes to creep about in it. A few larch or Scotch firs as a boundary to it are an advantage, as they give it a protecting fringe, and deter malicious people from setting fire to it. Five acres is plenty of extent for a gorse under any ordinary circumstances— and do not cut a ride in it. If it is larger, you may be tempted to divide it by a ride, so as to get foxes away more easily, and by doing so you will probably spoil it. I once did so, and never could rely on the covert again as a holding one. Do not make an artificial earth inside a gorse, for two reasons. It will be always difficult to get at to stop, and secondly you will have to be continually disturbing the covert to go to the earth and stop it. The smell of a man's foot within his sanctuary is worse than that of a dog, and is fatal to a fox's happiness. Have your earth outside in an adjoining wood or plantation. The worst of gorse coverts are that foxes, by the aid of rabbits, make earths in their midst, which you can seldom discover, and which, if you do, you dare not touch for fear of spoiling the covert. I had been aware of such an earth in a gorse of mine for years, which had cheated us of many a run, but I never saw the earth until after the gorse was burnt, and even then it was the home of a litter of cubs. Natural earths, however, are not so likely to be made in a covert such as this, where it is planted on pretty level ground. If on the side of a bank, like Peele's Gorse for instance, the place is sure to be honeycombed. In the exuberance of my youth, and hot-headed love for all that pertained to fox preservation, I once brought from Epsom Downs a lot of seedling gorse to plant in Wales. The late Mr. Studd, Lord of the Manor, was trying to rid the six mile hill of gorse, so as to improve the training gallops, and I obtained leave to take the yearling shoots, with which I planted a covert that I called "Derby Gorse," and a great success it was. As I write the mask of one of its heroes complacently looks at me, inspiring me with a remembrance of that 3rd of March, 1879, when he contributed so gloriously to our enjoyment. On looking through some note books of a loved one, who will never again cheer us with his company in these sub-lunary hunting fields, I chanced upon his account of this very run, and perhaps in such a hungry time as this any old crumb may be of comfort to your sporting readers that has a genuine ring about it; so that I may be forgiven if I quote his diary on this Derby Gorse fox. "Met at Pilleth. Found at once in Derby Gorse, Bob putting in on the west side. Away over the top with the hounds close at him, over Morris's ground, crossing the lane to the right of the Warren, where they checked, letting most of the field up who had got a bad start. Hannibal hit him down Gwernaffel Dingle, and down to the Gwalse Wood, where he had loitered, and we raced him away through the Frydd, and, turning down, crossed the Presteign road near the turnpike, and on to Farrington ground, by the Withy tree, and over the Meeting House Hill, past Carter's and over the Stone Wall Hill, down to Willey Lodge, where I thought we were going to catch him, as he almost passed through the foldyard. But this gallant fox was on, and over Harley's Mountain —a fearful pull for the horses, now reduced to five or six—across the big fields of the Farlands, to the Lingen road, about a mile below the village, then straight for Deerfold, almost reaching the top; but, being beaten, he turned down across the Wigmore Road, and into Gisburne's Wood. We viewed him as he entered the wood, and saw that he had no more go in him. The hounds drove him down to the back of old G's house, and killed him in the shrubbery. I was pretty delighted to see the end, *as it was the finest run I ever saw.* He was a three-year old dog fox, very large, and no tag. His point no doubt was Wigmore Rolls, just a mile or two beyond where he turned down from Deerfold. Distance ten miles straight, and fourteen to sixteen as we ran. Time one hour and fifteen minutes, with only one check. The hounds went splendidly in this trying run, though at times through awkward ground they got a little separated, but soon got together again. Barmaid, Duster, Druid, and Baffler, were in front a great part of the run. Also Warlike at the beginning. Old hounds, Barrister especially, and Bowman, Hannibal, and Harold, not in it."

Beckford says: "You ask at what time you should leave off hunting? It is a question which I know not how to answer, as it depends as much on the quantity of game that you have, as on the counties that you hunt. However, in my opinion, no good country should be hunted after February. Nor should there be any hunting at all after March. Spring hunting is sad destruction of foxes. In one week you may destroy as many as would have shown you sport for a whole season.

How long do you intend hunting? is a question often put to a master of the hounds.—Mr. Vyner's answer was "As long as the peas and beans will allow us." "'Ware wheat" in his opinion is a delusion. Old Ralph Lambton once late in a season broke up a fox in a wheat field, after a very good run, and was so ashamed of himself afterwards, that he sent the farmer a cheque for £10. When the harvest came round, he was astonished at having the money returned to him by the honest farmer, and being told by him that he had the best crop he ever saw on this field, That story has run through Yorkshire until it is a household word, and you seldom hear, "'Ware wheat" there.

Talking of killing foxes late in the season, it is a recorded fact that the Belvoir Hounds once on the 10th of April killed five old foxes, and thirteen or fourteen cubs. This is a feat unworthy of emulation. What Borderer keeps on saying, asleep and awake, is "shall we have a fair chance of trying to catch another fox this side August?" Perhaps not!

TWENTY FIRST WEEK, March 15th to 20th.

A welcome change. Gulliver in all his travels never came across such a transformation in scene, climate, and degree, than we have during the last three days. A Canadian winter breaks as suddenly, I believe, into Spring as we seem to be doing, but even in this changeful climate of ours few of us have experienced such an abandonment of extreme cold, and the presence of balmy Spring within the week.

The very sniff of the altered state of the atmosphere made sportsmen on Thursday night feel new men, and on Friday, come what might, Borderer felt compelled to be on a horse, just for a bit of exercise if for nothing else, to give the liver a turn, and risk being kicked off. The fog would be sure to clear by noon, and a stick found no resistance in the ground, except here and there. So to High Ercall he trotted, in solitary grandeur. Not a hunting coat on the broad horizon. Plenty of people bent on a sale at Mr. Lewis's of Roden, which I should hope was a success owing to the break-up of the frost. Thank goodness, there were Thatcher and the hounds at all events, even if the Shropshire people, excepting some score, had not awoken to the fact that hunting was practicable as soon as the fog cleared. Some shook their heads. "Impossible to ride." "Bosh, my friends, hounds can hunt, and follow them we must as best we can. Horses will jump all the better at the ditches full of snow, only don't ride too fast at them for fear of the take off being a trifle treacherous." About twelve o'clock out came old Sol, and away we went to draw Ercall Park, where very soon we had an holloa away, which when we arrived at the scene was pronounced to be a vixen, which the hounds on their part seemed as much disinclined to hunt as did the huntsman. The other coverts nearer the river were blank, and so was the Marle; it has not held a fox this year, and is thoroughly cut up and disturbed, so no one was disappointed. Forester's Plantation, too, followed suit, and there was nothing left but a move to Rowton Gorse. Never perhaps in the annals of Shropshire has such a small field gone down to take part in this draw. Not more than a score, all told, one half of which by common consent went to the further end next the railway, and the remainder waited at the foot of the hill, a field away, so that there should be no excuse for heading him. Still patiently we waited. Foxes were at home, but their stay at home propensities that have so often been the bane of this sweet little covert seemed as strong as ever. At last the first whip gives a faint cheer, and the quiet scene springs into life. A fox had broke at the top corner by the side of the brook, and hounds flashed up the meadow parallel with it. Our little cohort is divided, some on one side, and same on the other. It is a doubtful point which fortune will favour. Now they cross the brook to our side, and we waive a defiant "come on" to our friends on the other side. In another field they have the laugh at us, for hounds re-cross, and we have to be after them. Luckily, a ford is straight in front of us, and away we go prettily. Frost and snow are forgotten; the country rides safely enough. Our fox takes us still on the grass parallel with the railway and brook, a pretty line. Does he mean Wytheford? No; he leaves it to the left, and Ellerdine seems his point. Now there is the brook in earnest, and, as usual, second thoughts are worst. A Chestnut and a lady are over, but with the rest there is scrambling and grief, as the next field gives us a worse take-off and landing. Borderer flounders into a bog, a soldier mistakes a plank bridge for a safe means of crossing, and in goes his horse, luckily without damage. Hounds are accommodating in their pace, and do no run straight away from us, so that before Ellerdine is reached we are with them again. Here scent seems to desert us altogether, and it looks as if he has beaten us, but Thatcher's ideas of his whereabouts are right, he has turned back for Wytheford, in a little covert before reaching which he laid down. The first whip cleverly catches his eye on him, and hounds come out and race him in view into Wytheford Wood, through one corner of it, and out towards the Shawbury Road, one other dash into the wood and out again, only to be caught in the open, rather ignominiously as Borderer thought, although he proves an old fox, and is stiff as a crutch. This shows how the heavy state of the ground and long inactivity had told on our foe as much as upon ourselves. We had run him about forty minutes. Better than staying at home, we all agreed, for had we not warmed our blood, and seen a fox killed? Then ended the fun of the day, for there was no other fox in Wytheford, Morgan's Pool, or the Hazels. On Saturday, I believe, they were to go to the Hills from the Kennels, and I have not heard what befell. No can I give any later intelligence this week of Rednal or other places, having to be elsewhere, but I shall hope for a full budget for next week if all's well.

So the Wheatland are going back to their old management, and Mr. Turnbull is going to take the horn— a most plucky proceeding, considering his age. It is acknowledged on all hands that no one knows the country better than he does, nor is keener. To which he adds a natural aptitude for the work, which I think nobody else has attained to, and to which Borderer adds his blessing.

All the world will go to Liverpool to see the Grand National run this week, and it will seem like the palmy days of steeplechasing when at least twenty-five competitors will sport silk. My pet Ringlet has met with an accident, and Redpath is not so strong a favourite as I expected. My other chosen ones, Sinbad, Savoyard, and Gerona will run well, I think, but are in the outside division, while Ivanhoe will play second fiddle to the second favourite, Coronet, whom everybody tells me cannot be beaten. When called Prince Rudolph II. he certainly has not performed like such a good horse, but time will show. I dare not oppose him. I do not think

Mr. E. P. Wilson is destined to win it this year. His horses have too much weight, and the ground will be very heavy. There will be great cannonading in such a crowd, and I fear some nasty tumbles. The fittest horse with the lightest weight will come in front, and perhaps Old Badger will astonish the natives. The Irishmen all swear by Too Good. I never knew a horse too good for such a race as this, and the probability is that he will turn out *not good enough* at the end of the four miles and a quarter with 11st. 12lb. on his back. Amicia is just the sort of light-framed mare that will not stick in the dirt, and may be nearer first than last if Frank Cotton has got her as fit as she was last year at Ludlow. Borderer, however, is not in stables' secrets now, and will go with the tide in taking Coronet for the big steeplechase of the week.

TWENTY SECOND WEEK, MARCH 22ND TO 29TH.

Sir Watkin re-opened the ball at Maesfen on Saturday, the 20th ult., but spent the greater part of the day in or near the Wyches, which effectually took the gloss off the fresh horses, and put them and hounds into condition for Monday, when there was the usual throng at Rednal Station, and a rare hunting morning—too hot for choice. The high ground round Tedsmore was first tried, ineffectually ; and then a trot through Pradoe brought the calvacade to Sandford Pool, which also for a wonder was untenanted. A patch of gorse beyond, however, held a fox, and he preferred popping into a rabbit hole to affording sport. However, the persuasions of a terrier and spades were too conclusive for him, and away he went for West Felton and on to Pradoe, close to the church, then dipping down crossed the brook on to Shelvock Farm, and so on through the small covert between these and Grig Hill, which he reached, and went to ground after a pretty gallop—albeit a bit flashy —hounds running fast and slow by turns. Those that liked jumping had it, and those that chose to shirk saw a good deal of the run. While the fox was being dug out another was soon put going in the Ruyton Shrubberies. He lost no time in being off at the bottom, too quick indeed for the majority of the field, down towards Shotatton, before reaching which he turned to the right for the higher ground of Knockin Heath. Here a good old sportsman on his grey cob, the Rev. Mr. Tabor, came a terrible purler—a strong stake completely turned over both horse and rider, and when the horse rose there seemed no life in the prone form of the rider. Kind hands, including Sir Watkin, soon lifted him up, and the doctor, whose nags are always so near the front, was happily within call, so that what appeared like a dislocated neck was quickly screwed straight again. Mr. Tabor's tumbles have not been few, and we trust he will recover from this one as he has from others. He is made of stiffer materials than most of his cloth, and we can ill afford to lose him. All this time hounds were running well to Lord Bradford's Gorse, where they checked, and then went on to Sandford Pool, where he was headed back to the gorse and killed. Another enjoyable run for those who had not to assist in Mr. Tabor's accident. In the meantime the first fox had been unearthed, and was given another chance for his life, of which he failed to avail himself, and was killed in Grig Hill.

Another accident befell one of our best men last week. When out with Sir Watkin, Lord Alexander Paget accomplished the rather unusual feat for him of standing on his head, which rendered him unconscious for a time. We all rejoice to hear he is not much the worse.

Sporting papers have improved the occasion by announcing that, "Owing to numerous disappointments Sir Watkin will not hunt again till May!" and such is the gullibility of the daily papers that they have one and all copied this palpable absurdity.

On Tuesday, Mr. Corbet was as usual at Wrenbury with his crowd of followers. Broomhall was the first starting place, but the fox chose an awkward line with the river Weaver, the canal, and railway to be crossed, and did not afford much fun. Courts Gorse gave a short spin to ground near Aston. Then Combermere in the evening, when the bulk of pursuers had retreated to their trains, produced a sharp little gallop, the best of the day, to Burley Dam, over Bennett's Brook, and to ground at Brook's Mill, too soon to make it as good as it ought to have been had the fox gone straight or in the line he had chosen.

Wednesday, at Eaton Mascott, the Shropshire turned out in full strength, and the young squire, Mr. Wood, showed splendid hospitality. Unluckily, his home coverts had been disturbed by strolling dogs, and Goldings, for the first time this season, did not hold a fox. The Dole at Cound, however, was more fortunate. Here a brace were found. One broke over the railway for Eaton Mascott, the other, after some persuasion, got away down past Lower Cound to the river Severn, but he was not so amphibious as the last fox in that country, for he swung back to the left, and made a pretty circuit to Colton. Such nice clean-cut fences, sound on both sides, and no picking places. Shropshire jumping powder was to the fore. He then took them on to Brompton Wood, dodged about a bit here, and then went nearly to the Cross Houses, managing to elude his pursuers at the junction of the roads near the Eaton Mascott Lodge. A long blank draw ensued, Stevens Hill, Acton Burnell Park, and the Obelisk being the principal scenes of it. Pitchford, however, came to the rescue, and in the Birches Planting, a good fox was found that took the remnant of the field fast to Cantlop, and then sharp back to the left to the Clump, through the big wood, and on over Sir Frederick's model farm to the Obelisk, where they checked. Thatcher hunted him a few fields beyond, but failed to hit him towards Frodesley Hill, a couple of hounds having in the meantime taken the line towards Acton Burnell Park Wood —not an inviting place at five p.m.

On Thursday there were the dual attractions of Bettisfield with Sir Watkin, or Haughmond Abbey with the Shropshire. Let us take a peep at Bettisfield first. Sir E. Hanmer's foxes had betaken themselves by common consent to the Fens, which all the sporting world hereabouts knows is a part of Whixall Great Moss, and about as awkward a place for a bustling field as could well be imagined. Seven foxes were viewed away, some of them apparently taking good lines, but on none of these could the hounds be prevailed upon to come. Holloas and anathemas were useless. At last all the remaining foxes apparently made themselves scarce, and the master gave the word for Blackoe. Here some of the escaped ones had passed through, but stayed not. Iscoyd produced a vixen that was immediately chopped, while her better half in a most ungentlemanly way, went to ground before her very face. Kiln Green Wood was blank, and then we were at the Fens again. One stiff old fox that had had a good run on his own account was caught, and then at four p.m. Llanbedder Moss was ordered to be drawn. A fox was soon away, and gave us a nice twenty minutes to ground. So much for a very peaty day.

Haughmond Abbey failed to draw so large a field as usual, and what is worse, Holly Coppice did not hold a fox. There were two or three on the hill, however, and one of these, after a little badgering, essayed to go to Holly Coppice, but he was of a nervous temperament, and was flustered by an excellent sportsman's physiognomy in the road, so that he met his death in the bit of gorse close by. Another fox was poked out of a rabbit hole on the hill, and halloaed, but Thatcher was bent on Roden Coppice, which was blank, and also Poynton Springs, Ebury Wood, and Sunderton. The Gregories, however, made amends for much disappointment, as a fox broke to the south, skirting the Sundorne Decoy, crossed the main road to Pimley Rough, a most unusual line. Thatcher, before he reached here, had a nasty cropper at the brook; the old Colonel jumped short, and fell back into it. It looked as if the fox meant crossing the canal and river Severn to Monkmoor, but his intentions luckily were not so severe. He ran parallel with the canal back towards Shrewsbury. Those that liked big jumping had it; gates were handy for the remainder. When it looked as if he would enter the county town he turned to the right, re-crossed the main road, and went a capital line of grass back to Battlefield, just before reaching which came a check on the Shawbury road. Hitting him off, however, they ran up to Battlefield, where he dodged about,

LORD COMBERMERE (H. F. Mytton).

crossing and re-crossing the railway, quite beaten, and was eventually caught on the railway bridge, after a very nice run of an hour and seven minutes.

I am sorry to say that, although Thatcher re-mounted The Colonel, and the horse carried him wonderfully up to the check in the road, he there faltered, and was evidently injured inwardly, for he died that night. A great loss to the master, and a better hunter for a light weight never went into a field.

The Grand National monopolised the West Midlands on Friday, and never did a more exciting race ensue to rouse the enthusiasm of the assembled multitude. It is many years since twenty-three horses have competed. Few expected the Shrewsbury Autumn Hunt Steeplechase winner, Old Joe, to pull through, and yet he proved himself the best stayer of the lot. This will make us think more of our hunters after all. Old Joe had been the property of a Scotch huntsman, and had cost £30; but his blood is undeniable, being by Barefoot, a son of Lord Clifden's, out of a Stockwell mare, and his dam being by Chevalier D'Industrie, out of Truth by the Libel. One of my selections, Savoyard, would as nearly as possible have won had he not fallen at the last hurdle, as he has more speed than the winner. He is a son of the great New Oswestry. Gamecock, another fine hunter-like horse was third, and Too Good proved not quite good enough, as I expected, to win the trophy for the Irishmen, as he had to leather away in the rear of Old Joe throughout the journey. Our Cheshire mare, Amicia, was not quite so fit as she might have been, and her big trial so near the day no doubt upset her. Perhaps she will improve upon this form with time. She jumped the country, and beat more than beat her.

Borderer could not get to the Hawkestone Hills on Saturday, and reserves Baschurch (Monday) for the future. He might have added to these notes a day with the West Hereford at Pembridge Station, but here disappointment reigned supreme, so he hopes for better things ere these fine spring days have rung the knell of the season. "For one more week only," as the play bills say—and positively the sponge will have to be thrown up, except at the Wrekin and Longmynd.

TWENTY THIRD WEEK, MARCH 31ST TO APRIL 7TH.

Pilleth, in Radnorshire, has an historic interest. It was here that the Welsh and English tried conclusions many centuries ago, when Roger Mortimer had to take a licking from Owen Glyndwr—a feat that drove back the supremacy of the Lords of the Marches for many a long year out of this Border country. It was at Pilleth where Shakespeare has immortalised the cruel behaviour of the Welsh women over the bodies of those hated Englishmen.

Now all that is happily forgotten and forgiven. To-day we meet in good tempered rivalry with no ideas of Chevy Chase pervading us. Here come the descendants of Roger Mortimer—there is a Harley amongst them—a lineal representative of Oxford and Mortimer, and here are the Owen Glyndwrs of to-day—the representatives of those whose tombs in yonder little church carry us back to former centuries, when foxhunting was not preferred to fighting.

A curious old parish register hereabouts gives us a clue to the date when fox destruction was meritorious, and when the tide turned in the favour of foxhunting. Here are some extracts:—

In A.D. 1704 For killing a fox................................. 1/-
       1714 Paid Edward Lucas for digging out the fox 1/-
       1715 Killing two urchins, John Price......... 2d.
       1718 For destroying Kewotts 1/-
       1721 For ale when fox was killed 2/6
       1724 Mary Vaughan for expenses at killing Foxes... 2/6
             For killing six foxes 12/-
             Ditto two Foxes 5/-
       1725 Mary Vaughan for expenses of killing two foxes 10/6
       1730 For killing a fox 5/-
             Ale at ditto 2/6

This goes on up to 1800, when the practice ceases, and no doubt hunting began. These exploits came out of the Church rates, and no doubt Mary Vaughan kept the village public. Supposing we charged foxhunting on the rates now, how people would howl! Can any of your readers tell me what "Kewotts" are?

With this little bit of poaching on "Shreds and Patches," let us go forward to Monday, the 29th inst., at Pilleth, where Colonel Price led the van, and a gallant little army, including three Amazons, followed him in a day's warfare against the foxes of to-day.

Some nasty rain storms greeted us as we reached Ganders' Bridge Gorse, and gave us their company on to Weyman's Gorse, in neither of which generally safe places did our foe turn up. The rough night had kept him or them underground. So on we went, exceedingly damp and depressed, to Henewm Gorse on Whitton Hill. In this more sheltered spot hounds soon began to feather. At last one old one fairly stood and pointed at a brake of gorse not larger than a room. It was only for a moment, then in he dived, and out came a fox, like a Jack-in-the box, out of its very thickest part. He seemed to take in the situation at once, and down he went again—every hound in the pack surrounding him. Indeed escape seemed impossible. We held our breath in suspense. When suddenly out sprang a brace of foxes right over the backs of the astounded pack; as they struggled into the brake—a cleverer deliverance from seventeen couple of eager jaws I never saw. Each fox took different ways round detached gorse bushes, and in less than no time had cleared the pack, and were running away parallel to each other. Slipping through the wire fence they soon put a safe distance between themselves and the pack. Excuse me, dear readers, for dwelling for a minute or two over a scene that is indelibly painted on my memory. Those two grand dog foxes—long, light-coloured greyhounds; there seemed hardly a pin to choose between them for beauty and pace as they swept over the hill. One was a trifle larger than the other, and the smaller one had the biggest white tag on his brush. As they disappeared over the horizon it was time to catch hold of our horse's head, and begin the fray. The Norton coverts detained us not, nor did Knighton's Wood Gorse, although a fresh fox slipped back from there with a couple of hounds after him. Carter's Dingle was better for the hounds than the horses, but the knowing ones kept

the higher ground. At Bowen's hedges hounds hesitated
for a moment, but the Colonel soon put them right,
through the round fir clump. Stanage was left on
the left, Willey Lodge passed, and Harley's Mountain
partially climbed. Along its side, opposite Pedwardine
Wood they ran prettily, and down through Berkley Knoll.
Just an hour to this point, quite straight, said a trust-
worthy watch. Now came the second, or middle phase of
this great run. Turning to the right, above the main road,
we had to encounter ploughed land, sheep, and lots of
difficulties, past the Farlands, and then turned by a team
up the hill again, it took us nearly an hour to carry the
scent into the upper end of Lingen Valletts. Here to the
real hound lover was perhaps the greatest treat of the
day. Never lifted a yard, without a holloa or aid
of any kind, they had worked out their problem with
a patience and push that could not have been excelled.
Once in the Valletts scent slowly improved, until the
lower end in some thick briars our fox had waited.
Borderer heard the crash, and imagine his joy at viewing
him over the side, scarce fifty yards in front of the
pack! Yes, there he was, the self-same fine fellow
that had proudly waved defiance to us at the start,
but now he went stiff and high, his back was still straight,
but his coat was dirty, and had lost its gloss. I gave him
another ten minutes to live, and stirred up the well-bred
young Siderolite for another effort. Alas, the fallacy of
human calculations! Down towards the village he is
headed. Round the two hundred acre covert, and another
vain attempt to get away. We shall catch him. No, he
is over Coleshill, and out towards Kinsham. There are
two lines—hounds dash back towards the hill, but the
Colonel shakes his head ominously, his practised eye sees
that he is wrong, but who can stop hounds with tired
horses and up a hill? There is nothing for it but patience,
and here Colonel Price excels all other huntsmen I ever
saw. He gets to them at last, and returns to the spot,
where he thinks the mischief was done. The field in the
meantime have either been tailed off, or have lost heart at
this *contretemps*, for very few are with the master now.
Borderer confesses to the bitter compunction which
compelled him on reaching the top of Coleshill to decline

further contest. To kill a friend's horse would have been an alternative that, ardent as he is, he never could have benignly accomplished. So, sadly discontented, he turned homewards for a solitary twelve miles jog, cogitating over this great run, mentally deciding that this fox must be a lineal descendant of the old Norton wolf, a tremendous big fox that for several seasons had defied the hounds but was killed at last. Inquiries on the road told him that his friend was not in front, so he would probably pick him up *en route*. But he didn't. And long after B's legs had been under his mahogany—not till nine p.m.—did a familiar voice exclaim, " Why, what in the world became of you, B ? Here's his brush—pulled him down in the open—the same fox, I'll swear it, that we found at Henewm —killed him near Lyme brook—after running past Gisburne's, and up to Deerford Gorse, then to the finish nearly the whole way in view. Only three of us there besides the Colonel. Four hours altogether. Don't you call that a run ? " Yes I do, and if the result was not a triumph of the Welsh cross in hounds, aided by consummate judgment in the huntsman, over the best of foxes, Borderer does not know what verdict to pass on it. To compute the distance of this run is very difficult. To Berkeley Gate was a straight seven miles, afterwards there were many turns and windings, but measuring by time, we found a few minutes before one o'clock, and killed about five p.m., would make the distance much beyond twenty miles, and considering the deep state of the ground there can be little wonder that so few horses got to the end of it.

On Monday, the 29th, Sir Watkin at last brought off a Baschurch Monday, after many disappointments. The orders were for the Lordship, and nobody who witnessed that long cavalcade of well-appointed men and horses could gainsay the fact that Shropshire is a sporting county. Grafton Gorse was the first place of departure, and a fox was rattled away towards Montford Bridge, and then, wheeling to the right, touched a larch plantation of Earl Powis's, and was pushed on to Adcot, where, hard pressed, this poor lordly pug revisited the scene of his nightly depredations in the henroost, where Lockey soon acted as turnkey, and the pack executioned him. Mrs. Alfred Darby was revenged for the loss of her prize poultry. America now became the scene of operations. How our cousins across the Atlantic would rejoice if they had such a covert and such a sweet bit of galloping ground from it as here abounds. Lying in a wide bend of the Severn, near where the Verniew joins it, America gives a very smart fifteen minutes gallop to Nesscliff or anywhere else. To-day it held a fox that went away in good style, and afforded no end of fun until he managed to make his escape near the scene of the first fox's death. Nesscliff then became the order of the day, and my information goes no further.

At Loppington on this same Monday, the Shropshire had a long fruitless draw, and did not find until they reached Preston Gubbalds, from which they had a fast twenty-five minutes and killed.

Tuesday and Wednesday were days on which it was next to impossible to face the blustering and rainy elements. Consequently little or no sport could be expected from Leebotwood with the Shropshire, although a fox from the Lawley took them to Frodesley and Netherwood, and Mr. Corbett had a good run from Major Starkey's covert to Peckforton and Wardle, where he was killed in spite of the weather.

On Thursday, at the fifth milestone on the Baschurch Road, foxes did not seem plentiful. Perhaps the open earths accounted for this in a measure. Fitz Coppice, Leaton, and its surroundings failed to produce a fox. At last Merrington set the ball rolling towards Middle Park and Harmer Hill, where a brace were on foot, and hounds divided—one lot going towards Broughton Gorse, and the other the opposite way. In the result, both foxes were soon lost, and a poor day came to an end.

The familiar form of the old Leaton grey will never again show us how the Shropshire country should be crossed. He came to grief in a big run with the Cheshire on Friday, and was gently laid to his rest. As his owner truly says, "As good a one many men may have had; a better, never." His almost faultless form was immortalised I rejoice to say, in a sketch in these notes last season, and those in search of a hunter will not do amiss to carry in eye this combination of power, pluck, and perfection, such as were marked in this grand old hunter that had seen well nigh twenty summers.

Bangor Steeplechases, on Friday, were favoured with fine weather, but I understand failed to create as much fun and enthusiasm as usual. It was feared that the floods of the Dee would put a stop to them, but this, happily, was not the case. It was pleasing to see a Wynn still to the front, a most promising horseman, and of course the Ash stable scored a win to keep the people in a good humour.

On Thursday and Friday, Shrewsbury Spring Meeting is to be brought off, when I trust there will be good sport to tempt sportsmen from all round the Wrekin. The entries give promise of fair fields.

In the Shrewsbury Spring Handicap I like the looks of Craig Royston and Oliver Twist. In the Severn Plate, Boundary. The Bradford Two-year-old Plate has a lot of dark entries, except Binder, who has 12-lb extra to carry, but perhaps Mr. Abington will have a second string in Warble good enough; or Mr. Jousiffe's filly by Reverberation, out of Perea, may be smart. In the Borough Open Hunt Steeplechases, Chancellor looks rosy. In the Shropshire Hunt Cup we will take the Jones nominations against the remainder, unless the Cow can land it without the three acres! while the Private Sweepstakes may go to Leaton Knolls.

On Friday Silver Sea or Edward should win the Apley Welter, the Countess or Oliver Twist the Acton Burnell Handicap, Prince Io or the Wrekin the Hawkestone Handicap, and Chancellor or Coracle the Tradesmen's Hunt Steeplechase.

Can it be true that there is a transmigration of souls —I beg pardon, I mean of cubs—from Shropshire into more fashionable countries? Such things seldom carry with them a blessing. A change of blood is not a bad thing, and I hope there will be a corresponding return of cubs from the more fashionable countries, just to make things square. The exportation of foxes will soon get carried too far. M.F.H.'s, like other mortals, hate to be robbed. A man not satisfied with taking his stud of horses must needs import his foxes also—as well as his champagnes:—

> O Nimium. creed Judæus—ab illo
> O tempora, O mores!

Shropshire farmers may go farther and fare worse than in patronising a shire horse, the property of Mr. P. Muntz, M.P., called "Surprise," that I had the pleasure of looking over to-day at Shrewsbury. A first-rate specimen of a powerful short-legged cart horse, such as is sure to improve the breed wherever he goes. I congratulate the county on his acquisition.

And now my notes must come to an end. The season for all practical purposes is done. I wish it had told a more flattering tale. We sportsmen are not unaccustomed to failures and disappointments, and, therefore, are able to bear like true Britons this short, frost-bound, bad scenting season, grateful that there is much to look forward to, a few pleasant glimpses in the past, and many hopeful signs in the future. There is not one cloud on the horizon which threatens us with real dangers. Birds of evil omen croak faintly, but we heed them not, knowing that our West Midland Chronicle is likely to survive many an angry scare, and many an imaginary difficulty.

I have endeavoured to hold "the mirror up to nature," and if the picture has not alway been so fair to look upon as the keenest among us could have wished, do not let us forget Pope's truthful essay on criticism, wherein he says,

> Whoever thinks a faultless piece to see.
> Thinks what ne'er was, nor is, nor e'er shall be.

Once more I have been persuaded to publish these notes accompanied by some portraits of local interest, and with sketches by Mr. H. F. Mytton, which will mark some of the incidents herein detailed. They at least will help to redeem the monotony of an oft told tale, and carry with them, I trust, a few sweet remembrances of a winter's sport. On the principle of *Bis dat qui cito dat* we intend the publication to be made within a few days, and to it will be added something of a useful nature as an index to hospitable quarters. Sporting tradesmen, the best shops, and other information beneficial to our county town and my readers. "All for the honour of Shropshire!" Adieu!

INDEX.

ACCIDENTS ... 16. 30. 37, 40, 41, 92, 57, 63, 70	Bettisfield 15, 93
Acton Reynald 9. 36	Bibby, Mr. Frank ... 67
Acton Burnell 63, 93	Biddulph Miss, Marriage of 8
Adderley... ... ... 27, 25	Boughey, Lady. Picture 14
Adcot 99	Boxing Day 29. 31
Alexander Paget, Lord... 92	CARDEN 35, 69
Albrighton Hall... ... 41, 77	Cheshire, South... ... 23
Aldersey 17	Cholmondeley 23
Almeley Village... ... 11	Cholmondeley Lady's Accident 41
Ash Gorse 26	Church Stretton ... 34
Atcham Bridge 10, 42	Combermere 92
Aston 92	Colonel, The 95
BALL, the Hunt... ... 9, 42	Condover Hall 58
Bangor Steeplechases ... 101	Corbet, Sir Vincent ... 37
Barclay Mrs., Marriage... 8	Coton Hall 11, 37
Baschurch... 9, 20, 36, 37. 68, 95, 99	Cotes, Colonel 44
Battlefield 29, 94	Cressage 71
Beavan, Henry 3	Croome, The 39
Beckford 87	Cub Hunting 3
Berwick Hall 7, 41	Culmington Manor ... 39

INDEX.

Derby Gorse	86
Dorrington Station ...	16. 27
Eaton Mascott ...	93
Ellerdine	89
Felton, West	21, 91
Fifth Milestone...	66, 100
Fox Killing out of Church Rates ...	96
Fox Terrier Show ...	22
Fox in a Tree	33
Frodesley	100
Gentleman in Black	45
Golding's Coppice ...	64
Gnosall	70
Goosehill Run, The ...	74
Gorse Coverts, new ...	85
Grand National ...	90, 95
Grand National Hunt Steeplechase	22, 83
Gresford	24
Grigg Hill ...	22, 91
Habits, Ladies'... ...	46
Habits, Gentleman's ...	51
Harley, Mr.	96
Harrop, Hulton, Mr. ...	72
Hardwicke	17, 67
Haughmond Abbey	59, 93, 94
Herefordshire West ...	11, 95
Henewm Gorse ...	97
High Ercall ...	24, 31, 88
Hill, the late Mrs. Clement	8
Hindlip, Lord	74
Hinton	25, 58
Hunter's Sale	83
Huntington	11
Iscoyd	31, 75, 94
Kennels, The ...	36, 90
King Nip	77
Kinsham	98
Knockin Heath... ...	92
Kyre	39
Leaton	28, 100
Leebotwood	100
Liverpool	90
Lloyd, Lady Frances, the late	57
Lockey, Will	2, 20
Loppington	57
Losford	39
Loton Park	24, 39
Lythwood	6, 54
Maesfen	91
Merrington	61
Middle Village	19
Montford Bridge ...	69, 99
Muntz, Mr., M.P. ...	102
Nesscliff	100
Newcastle	19
New Street Lane ...	28, 71
Nimrod	61, 65
Norton Manor	36
Offley Grove ...	6
Old Joe	5, 95
Onibury Station ...	62
Onslow	70
Oteley	57
Overton Bridge... ...	41
Owen Glyndwr... ...	96
Pedwardine Wood ...	98
Petton	36, 93
Pilleth	64, 96
Pitchford ...	43, 39, 63

Pointon Springs	... 81, 91	Styche	... ...	28
Politics	... 23	Sutton, Sir Richard	...	37
Prees Station ...	... 26	Swann, Robert, Marriage		15
Preston Gubbald,	17, 30, 19, 100	THATCHER'S FALL	...	12
Price, Colonel ...	... 97	Tugford	...	39
RACES, Shrewsbury	4, 40, 101	Twemlows	... ...	26
Radnorshire ...	36, 64, 97	UNITED, The ...	... 19, 34	
Rates, Old Church	... 96	WALFORD	... ...	28
Rednal	... 91	Welsh Hounds ...	...	66
Rowton Gorse ...	... 34, 69	Welshpool Stag Hunt	...	11
SANDFORD POOL	... 21, 91	Wem Station ...	...	12
Severn Crossing	... 72	Weston Heath ...	...	85
Shawbury ...	13, 59, 70	Weston	...	54
Shottatton ...	... 21, 92	Westminster, Duchess,		
Sir Watkin, the late	... 2	Accident ...	...	40
Skinner, Eli ...	... 57	Wheatland, The	18, 35, 54, 90	
South Shropshire Country	73	Whitchurch Racecourse	5, 54	
Snow, Hunting in the	55	Whittington ...	...	33
Staghunt ...	... 11	Wicksted, Mr. C., Retire-		
Steeplechases, Bangor	83, 101	ment	59, 80, 82	
Starkey, Major, Gorse ...	69	Wilbrighton ...	...	10
Stapleton Village	... 76	Woore	... 32, 78	
Stafford, North...	... 32	Worcestershire, The	...	74
Stanwardine Gorse	... 13, 62	Wrenbury ...	9, 23, 38, 92	
Strefford's Bridge	... 6	Wrekin, The	... ...	81

Printed at the Office of "Eddowes's Shrewsbury Journal," Shrewsbury.

APPENDIX.

A SPORTSMAN'S Compendium to such a little work as this strikes the Author as not altogether out of place, and he has therefore got together some particulars of where sporting things can be obtained in their best qualities, as well as information to his readers, who may be strangers to Shropshire, in their search after the whereabouts of the best Hotels, Tradesmen, &c. To begin with there is the historic old Coaching House, the 'Lion' Hotel, where in the days of the 'Wonder,' everybody frequented, and wnere still every inducement is held out by its present proprietor. Mr. Fleet, to make people happy and comfortable. Here Jack Mytton was always at home. Its ball-room floor is of charmingly polished old oak, that has delighted the heart of many a thousand young *débutant*. May its surface never grow rougher! There is another Hotel which Borderer can personally recommend, that has just gone into fresh hands, a nice drive from the County Town, the ' Elephant and Castle,' at Shawbury. Mr. Hawkings is sure to please you. The 'Raven,' at Droitwich, too, is probably the most comfortable of its kind in Worcestershire. For rheumatism or gout, try Droitwich, says Dr. B, and if the 'Raven' does not please you, nothing else will at Droitwich, he can assure you.

And now as to Shrewsbury itself. Very few County Towns that I know of possess greater attractions to the sportsman. You need not think of sending to London for anything. If you want the best saddlery that the world can produce, go to Harries, in High Street. If you want to be booted and spurred, try his next door neighbour, Mr. Grant. If you want your trophies of the chase, gun, or rifle set up in a style that will be life-like and lasting, or if you want the finest of flies, tackle, or rods, go over the way to Mr. Shaw. If you want a silversmith or jeweller, talented, tasteful, and tempting. particularly his hunting watch, try Mr. Robinson, also in High Street. If you want a fishmonger fit to cope with Grove or Charles. try Messrs. F. & T. Hammond, of Castle Street. If you want a good gun maker, anxious to please, and well knowing his business, try Mr. S. Smallwood, of Mardol. If you want to be photographed in a style not second to Regent Street, visit Mr. La'ng's studio, in Castle Street, and you will not come away disappointed. If you want a good wine merchant, having found out the short-comings of your swell London man, go to Messrs. Thomas Southam & Sons, of Wyle Cop, and you will find all that you require—at least Borderer does. If you want to sell horses or carriages try Messrs. Hall, Wateridge & Owen. If you want to sell or buy sheep, cattle, or farming stock, where can you find the superiors of Messrs. Lythall, Mansell & Walters? If you want to hire a hunter for a gallop in Shropshire, Mr. Franklin, at the 'Raven,' takes pains to supply you. If you want to furnish a new house, and reside in the County, or indeed if you want a house, furniture, or anything appertaining thereto, you cannot do better than go to those civil, obliging tradesmen, Messrs. Blower, of Pride Hill. While in the matters of books and stationery, Messrs. Adnit & Naunton, in the Square, are equal to the occasion. In second-hand literature (especially in Borderer's unfortunate first series of Hunting Notes) Mr. Bennett of Mardol has all you want. Mr. C. A. Partridge, of Ludlow, is quite A 1. in every department, but makes a specialty of his sporting books--the best editions. Of local thoroughbred sires I am pleased to say that we can turn out some that will do honour to Shropshire. Read the pedigrees and performances of those that appear in the following pages, Linnæus, Polardine and Traveller, and if you are not eager to start breeding hunters Borderer will be astonished. If you want a thoroughly good sporting paper free from cant and humbug order forthwith " Horse and Hounds." No country gentleman can invest 2d per week to greater advantage. The Shrewsbury racecourse under its new management needs patronage and encouragement. The plan of the property will show how many capabilities it has and how anxious its managers are to fall in with the sporting views of the town and county of Salop.

There is some affinity, I suppose, between the Ludlow Dhu Stone and those disagreeable things called corns. Anyhow Mr. Alfred Marston, of Ludlow, claims to have a sovereign remedy. Try it My *universal provider* list is not yet exhausted. The illustrations of this book deserve a word or two. The portraits have been engraved from photos by a new process, which would appear to be capable of giving all the softness and delicacy of the finest steel plate engravings. I recently saw some wash drawings, paintings, engravings, &c., which for delicacy of finish left nothing to be desired. This process is worked by the Meisenbach Co., Limited, 31, Farringdon Street, London, E.C.—as have also Mr. H. F. Mytton's sketches.

THE RAVEN FAMILY HOTEL,

NEAR THE BRINE BATHS.

DROITWICH.

(In the centre of the Worcestershire Hunt.)

VERY GOOD STABLING.

Boarding Terms:

£3 10s. per week, including Meals, Bedroom, and attendance, with use of Public Rooms.

Dinner, Table d' Hote daily, 7 p.m. Meals taken in private Room or separately charged accordingly.

Sitting Room Fire, 1/6 per day. Bed Room Fire, evening only, 1/-.

Visitors' Servants, 5/- per day (including Ale); Bedroom, 1/6.

The Hotel, which is very pleasantly situated, contains good Coffee Room, Ladies' Drawing Room, Private Sitting Rooms, from 5/- per day; Large Airy Bed Rooms, from 2/6 per day, overlooking Gardens and Grounds for Lawn Tennis, &c. Also Billiard and Smoking Room.

GEORGE BUDDLE,
PROPRIETOR.

THE LION HOTEL, SHREWSBURY,

Oldest Established in the Town,

TOP OF THE WYLE COP.

Plenty of Accommodation and Comfort for Man and Horse.

HEAD QUARTERS OF THE YEOMANRY, CYCLING CLUB & FREE MASONS'

BEST BALL AND BILLIARD ROOMS.

Proprietor :—Mr. CHARLES FLEET.

Copies of the first edition ('84-'85) of

"HUNTING NOTES"

May be obtained as below, he having purchased the remaining Copies.

JOHN BENNETT,

BOOKSELLER, DEALER IN OIL PAINTINGS,

Engravings, Old China & Curiosities,

58 & 62. MARDOL, SHREWSBURY.

H. FRANKLIN,

Raven Stables and Cross Hill,

SHREWSBURY.

Hunters hired by the Day, Week, or Month.

POSTING IN ALL ITS BRANCHES.

LOOSE BOXES.   LIVERY AND BAIT STABLES.

TERMS MODERATE.

J. LAING,

CASTLE STREET, SHREWSBURY,

Photographer & Miniature Painter,

PHOTOGRAPHIC & FINE ART GALLERIES.

Family and Presentation Portraits from Locket Miniatures to Life Size, in Oil and Water Colours, executed by First-class Artists on the Premises.

MEDALS AWARDED FOR PHOTOGRAPHS OF HIGH ARTISTIC MERIT.

THE "COUNTY" FRAMING & GILDING ESTABLISHMENT.

Paintings re-lined & restored in an artistic manner.

ENGRAVINGS AND DRAWINGS CLEANED AND RESTORED.

EXPERIENCED OPERATORS SENT ANY DISTANCE TO PHOTOGRAPH VIEWS, HORSES, DOGS, GROUPS, &c., &c.

Artists' Materials at London Prices.

SAMUEL SMALLWOOD,
(From Westley Richards,)

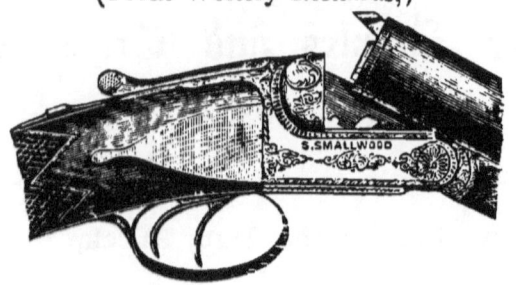

Manufacturer of every description of

BREECH AND MUZZLE-LOADING GUNS, RIFLES, PISTOLS, &c,

4 & 5, MARDOL, SHREWSBURY.

By Appointment Armourer Sergeant to Shropshire Yeomanry Cavalry.

Schultz, E. C. and Black Powder Cartridges at the lowest London Prices for Cash.

ALL KINDS OF AMMUNITION, IMPLEMENTS, ETC.

Repairs punctually attended to at most reasonable terms.

N.B.—Muzzle Loaders converted into Breech Loaders on the Newest Principle.

CORNS! CORNS!

ALFRED MARSTON, Chemist, LUDLOW,

Discovered in January, 1881. A CERTAIN CURE for these painful excrescences, which is quite different from any other preparation. It contains no caustic, acids, or anything irritating, and can be used with the greatest safety. As soon as the remedy is applied it forms a PLASTER ON THE CORN, keeps off all pressure, and gives immediate relief. **It is also a positive cure for Warts and Bunions.**

Read the following Testimonials, selected from thousands, received as a proof of its remarkable efficacy; the originals can be seen if required.

Sir, Strefford, January 21st, 1882.

Your **Corn Eradicator** has been quite successful in the case of all my patients who have used it. Yours sincerely, E. TREDINNICK, M.D.

"Kelvedon,' Gordon Road, Bournemouth, July 27th, 1885.

Dear Sir,—Will you please send me a bottle of your **Corn Eradicator**, for which I enclose Postal Order. I obtained a bottle of the above at Baker's Piazza di Spagna, Rome, last year, and found it much more efficacious than the Celandine and other preparations.

You are at perfect liberty to make whatever use you please of my letter. I shall be glad if it should induce any fellow sufferers to give the **Corn Eradicator** a trial, as they would be sure to thank me for the recommendation.

Yours truly, CHARLES F. JARVIS.

☞ THIS IS THE ORIGINAL AND ONLY GENUINE.

PRICES 9½d. and 1½d. PER BOTTLE.

PREPARED ONLY BY THE INVENTOR,

ALFRED MARSTON, Chemist, LUDLOW.

⇒ Alexander Grant, ⇐

BOOT AND SHOE MAKER,

4, HIGH STREET, SHREWSBURY.

Maker of all kinds of Ladies' and Gentlemen's Riding, Walking, and Shooting Boots.

Patent Dress "Court," and Evening Shoes kept in Stock.

Gentleman's Superior Hunting Boots made to order, and Servants Boots as supplied to the different Hunts in this and the adjoining Counties.

Boot-Trees for Riding and Shooting Boots made on the shortest Notice.

C. A. PARTRIDGE,
BROAD STREET, LUDLOW.

SPORTING NOVELS,

THE LARGEST STOCK IN THE COUNTY.

ORIGINAL AND NEW EDITIONS.

BADMINTON LIBRARY AS PUBLISHED.

THE
Elephant and Castle Hotel,
SHAWBURY.

MR. SELWYN HAWKINS,
PROPRIETOR.

CONTAINS EVERY COMFORT FOR SPORTSMEN OR TOURISTS.

Shawbury lies in the centre of North Shropshire; 4 Miles from Hadnal Station; 7 from Shrewsbury; 4 from Lea Bridge Kennels.

EXCELLENT STABLING. GOOD TROUT FISHING IN THE RIVER RODEN.

CARPETS! CURTAINS! LINOLEUMS!

Upholstery & Cabinet Show-rooms,

(LARGEST IN THE MIDLANDS.)

J. & B. BLOWER,

28, 29, 30, PRIDE HILL, SHREWSBURY,

DEALERS IN

MODERN & ANTIQUE FURNITURE, &c.,

Valuers, and House and Commission Agents.

Experienced Workmen, in every branch, sent to all parts, on the shortest notice.

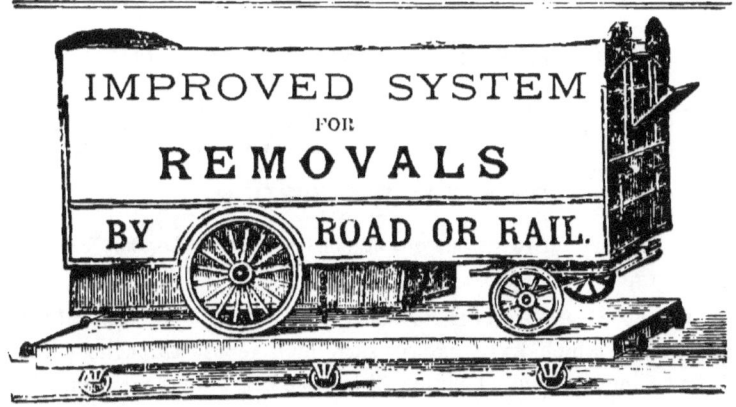

SHREWSBURY REPOSITORY,

Specially built for Storing Furniture and Valuables,

CASTLE GATES.

Estimates Free on Application.

THE MIDLAND COUNTIES
SADDLERY DEPOT,
HIGH STREET, SHREWSBURY.

G. E. HARRIES

BEGS respectfully to thank the Nobility and Gentry of this and the adjoining Counties for the extensive patronage bestowed on him for upwards of TWENTY YEARS, and solicits a continuance of the same.

Having largely increased his Staff of Workmen he is enabled to Manufacture on the premises, and under his own personal supervision

A LARGE & SUPERIOR STOCK OF
HIGH-CLASS SADDLERY,
OF EVERY DESCRIPTION,

Which he can offer to his patrons 20 per cent. under London Prices; and of a quality not to be excelled.

G. E. HARRIES begs to call attention to his HUNTING SADDLES, which have gained such high repute throughout the United Kingdom, and which it will ever be his study to maintain.

HORSES CAREFULLY FITTED, BOTH FOR GENTLEMEN'S & LADY'S SADDLES.

Horses Measured & Estimates given for every description of Harness.

1886.

THE THOROUGH-BRED SIRE
LINNAEUS
(FOALED 1878),
THE PROPERTY OF Mr. W. E. LITT.

A Grey Horse, standing 15-3 high, on very short legs, with great bone and power.

He is by Strathconan, out of Sweet Violet, by Voltigeur; out of Cowslip, by Oxford; out of Sweet Pea, by Touchstone; Strathconan, by Newminster.

LINNÆUS was one of the fastest horses of his day, and won many races, carrying heavy weights and beating large fields, generally in a canter. Amongst many other races which Linnæus won are the following:—

>The Oldham Welter, at Manchester, Sept. 1881.
>The Stewards' Cup, at Liverpool, Nov. 188 .
>The New Barns Handicap, at Manchester, April 1882.
>The Heaton Park Welter, at Manchester, Sept. 1882.
>The Craven Handicap, at Four Oaks, Oct. 1882.
>The Croxteth Cup, at Liverpool, Nov. 1882.
>The Leamington Plate, at Warwick, 1883.
>etc.   etc.   etc.

With his fine racing blood and great bone Linnæus is bound to get weight-carrying hunters, with plenty of quality, as he is a very handsome Horse himself, and perfectly sound.

He will serve thorough-bred Mares at 10 Guineas, and one Guinea Groom's Fee; and half-bred Mares at 3 Guineas, and 5s. the Groom Approved Mares the *bona fide* property of Tenant Farmers at 3 guineas, and 5s. the Groom.

Roomy Paddocks and Loose Boxes for Mares and Foals, with every possible attention at Ordinary Prices.

At Mr. **LITT'S STABLES,**
CROSS HILL,
SHREWSBURY.

F. & T. HAMMONDS,

FISHMONGERS,

FRUITERERS & GAME DEALERS,

CASTLE STREET,

✤ SHREWSBURY. ✤

A daily supply of all Kinds of Fish in Season from London and other Markets.

Address for Telegrams:—"ROBINSON. SHREWSBURY."

HENRY ROBINSON,

SILVERSMITH AND JEWELLER,

HIGH STREET, SHREWSBURY.

ANTIQUE PLATE:—A Large Collection of Genuine Specimens.

Silver Purchased, Exchanged, or Repaired.

VALUATIONS MADE.

COLLECTIONS INVENTORIED, DATED & DESCRIBED.

Specialities & Novelties for Wedding Gifts & Presentation.

DIAMONDS REMOUNTED.

The Longines Keyless Lever Huntsman's Watch, 42s., a marvel of strength, appearance and correct timekeeping.

High Street, SHREWSBURY.

MESSRS.

Wm. HALL, WATERIDGE & OWEN,

AUCTIONEERS AND VALUERS,

SHREWSBURY.

SALES OF ESTATES, TIMBER,

HOUSE PROPERTY, FARMING STOCK,

Household Furniture, Building Plant

MACHINERY, ETC., CONDUCTED.

VALUATIONS made for the Purpose of SALES, MORTGAGE or PROBATE.

AGRICULTURAL VALUERS & ARBITRATORS.

SMITHFIELD.—

SALE OF LIVE STOCK EVERY TUESDAY

THROUGHOUT THE YEAR.

HORSE SALES

AT THE RAVEN REPOSITORY

FOR

HUNTERS, CARRIAGE HORSES, HACKS, AND DRAUGHT HORSES,

The last Saturday in each Month.

CARRIAGE & HARNESS SALES QUARTERLY.

OFFICES:

BELMONT, SHREWSBURY.

ESTABLISHED 200 YEARS.

ADNITT AND NAUNTON,

BOOKSELLERS AND BOOKBINDERS,

GENERAL STATIONERS, ARTISTS' COLOURMEN.

Letterpress & Lithgraphic Printers,

Copper-plate Engravers, Colour Stampers, &c.

ALL NEW BOOKS RECEIVED IMMEDIATELY AFTER PUBLICATION.
2d. IN THE **1s.** DISCOUNT FOR CASH.

Books Bound in every Description of Plain and Elegant Bindings on the Premises, at London Prices.

A LARGE STOCK OF STATIONERY

OF ALL QUALITIES AND PRICES.

PRAYER BOOKS, CHURCH SERVICES, HYMN BOOKS, ETC., IN VARIOUS BINDINGS.

Oil and Water Colours & Drawing Materials of all kinds kept in Stock.

FANCY COLOUR LETTER-PRESS PRINTING

AS WELL AS

GENERAL & COMMERCIAL WORK,

OF SUPERIOR QUALITY.

At the lowest remunerating prices, combined with due regard to quality by Fast Printing Machines.

LITHOGRAPHIC & COPPER-PLATE PRINTING

EXECUTED IN THE FIRST STYLE OF ART.

Show Cards, Labels, etc., Printed in Gold or Colours.

THE SQUARE, SHREWSBURY.

AT LYTHWOOD HALL FARM,
THREE MILES FROM SHREWSBURY.

POLARDINE,
By "BEADSMAN," out of "REGALIA,"

Winner of Second Prize at the Hunters' Improvement Society's Show, March, 1886, where he was passed sound by Professor Axe, M.R.C.V.S., and two other Veterinary Surgeons, beating "Knight of the Launde" and "Pedometer." First and Second at the Royal Agricultural Show at Preston, 1885; "Marmion." First at the Shropshire and West Midland Show at Knighton, 1885, and twenty others.

Thoroughbreds, £5 5s.; Half do., £3 3s.; Tenant Farmers, £2 2s. (10s. deducted if paid within a week from first time of serving): Owner's Tenants, Free.

Apply T. RAWBONE,
Stud Groom,
Lythwood Hall, Shrewsbury.

1886.
THOROUGH-BRED STALLION
"TRAVELLER,"
SIX YEARS OLD,

By "Adventurer" out of "Acropolis," by "Citadel," her dam "Celina," by "Newminster," out of "Queen Bee," by "Amorino."

A limited number of Mares at £5 each and 5s. grooms fee. Mares *bonâ fide* the property of tenant farmers resident in the County hunted by Mr. A. P. Heywood-Lonsdale, gratis, except 5s. groom's fee. Mares the property of other tenant farmers £2 10s. and 5s. groom's fee.

For further particulars apply to
MR. F. STEVENS,
Lee Bridge Kennels,
Preston Brockhurst Shrewsbury.
THREE MILES FROM WEM STATION.

All Fees to be Prepaid.

"HORSE & HOUND."

A JOURNAL OF
SPORT AND AGRICULTURE.

CONTAINS

TATTERSALL'S FULL CATALOGUE;

TOWN AND COUNTRY GOSSIP:

ARTICLES BY "AUDAX," "BEACON," "DRAGON,"

"BORDERER," AND OTHERS:

HORSE SALES;

GENERAL NEWS.

PRICE TWOPENCE.

PUBLISHED BY

J. D. MACFARLANE,

14, Catherine Street, Strand.

DINNER WINES
At 24/- Per Doz.

Shipped direct from the countries of produce, and all of the purest and finest quality obtained.

"LA VINA" DINNER SHERRY.
"PALMA SPECIAL" NATURAL SHERRY.
PALE OR GOLD MADEIRA.
FINEST OLD VIRGIN MARSALA.
EXCELLENT ST. ESTEPHE CLARET.
SOUND STILL BURGUNDY.
NIERSTEINER STILL HOCK.
DELICATE STILL MOSELLE.
GOOD LIGHT SPARKLING MOSELLE.
PURE AND GOOD SPARKLING SAUMUR.

CARRIAGE FREE TO ALL STATIONS.

T. SOUTHAM & SONS, Wine Importers, Shrewsbury

Agents for BASS & CO., Burton; WATKINS & CO., Dublin; OLD SALOP BREWERY, &c.

Salop Stationery Stores,

WHOLESALE & RETAIL.

GENERAL PRINTING WORKS,

7, THE SQUARE, SHREWSBURY.

EVERY ARTICLE IN THE STATIONERY TRADE OF BEST QUALITY, AND AT LOWEST CASH PRICES.

Illuminated Addresses executed in the highest style of Art.

LETTERPRESS & LITHOGRAPHIC PRINTING, EMBOSSING & DIE SINKING.

GOOD WORK GUARANTEED.   PRICES LOW.

To Farmers, Breeders, and Exporters of High-class Cattle, Sheep, and Pigs.

MESSRS.

LYTHALL, MANSELL & WALTERS,

Secretaries to the Shropshire Sheep Breeders' Association & Flock Book Society,

AGRICULTURAL AUCTIONEERS, VALUERS, AND ESTATE AGENTS,

UNDERTAKE SALES OF HIGH-CLASS

FARMING STOCK

In any part of the Kingdom, and from their extensive connection can, at the shortest notice, execute commissions for any description of BRITISH STOCK, especially SHORTHORN CATTLE and SHROPSHIRE SHEEP. They have excellent accommodation for collecting together and keeping Stock prior to shipment. The highest references can be given in England, Scotland, Ireland, France, Germany, Austria, Algiers, North and South America, &c.

WEEKLY SALES AT SHREWSBURY & OSWESTRY OF

FAT AND STORE STOCK

EVERY TUESDAY & WEDNESDAY.

PERIODICAL SALES OF PURE-BRED

CATTLE, SHEEP AND PIGS,

HELD IN

BINGLEY HALL, BIRMINGHAM,

And Special Days arranged when a Sale at home is not desired.

Lichfield Public Cattle Sales Company.

Messrs. LYTHALL, MANSELL & WALTERS having been appointed Managers and Auctioneers, will hold FORTNIGHTLY SALES of Fat and Store Stock, Farm Produce, &c., in the Smithfield, Lichfield.

PERIODICAL SALES OF FAT & STORE STOCK, ETC., ARE ALSO HELD AT SUTTON COLDFIELD.

2,500 Shropshire Rams, and 20,000 Shropshire Ewes for Sale by Auction in the Autumn of 1886.

OFFICES—*College Hill, Shrewsbury; Bingley Hall, Birmingham; and 10, Salop Road, Oswestry.*

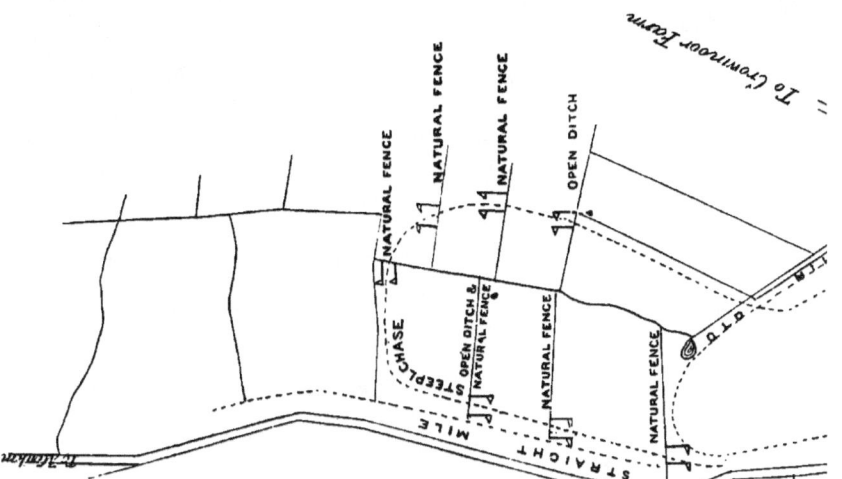

www.ingramcontent.com/pod-product-compliance
Lightning Source LLC
Chambersburg PA
CBHW020248170426

43202CB00008B/271